Even
Moses
Needed
Encouragement

15 Stories of Encouragement from the Bible

ILYNMW Publishing
Atlanta Georgia

Dedication

This book is dedicated to my Bride and the love of my life - Debbie.   In addition, I want to dedicate this book to my children - Hannah, David, Sarah and Jonathan. I am so proud of you guys and I love you no matter what!

I would also like to thank my Sunday school teacher Shane Eller who gave me the opportunity to first teach a lesson on encouragement to our class. It was out of this lesson that I had the inspiration for this book.   Shane is an incredible teacher, leader and encourager and I praise God that we are able to sit under his teaching.

Finally I want to thank by brother Jerry Davison who was there for me when I was "in the wilderness" and offered encouragement as well as some great ideas that helped to make this a better book.

Books by Paul Beersdorf

Flowers on Tuesday

52 Things I Wish My Father Had Taught Me about Marriage and Family

The 100 Most Important Words

Encouraging Your Wife

Encouraging Your Husband

Advice for Today, Tomorrow and Forever

Contents

Acknowledgements

I love my Bride and how much she encourages me to write and share my thoughts and ideas.   She is the love of my life and my best friend. Nothing I do would be worthwhile without her by my side.

I also want to thank all those men who consistently offer words of encouragement in my life.   There are too many to name and I don't want to leave anyone out, but you guys know who you are!!

Introduction

Definition - *Encouragement - something that makes someone more determined, hopeful, or confident*

I have heard it said that we should speak words of encouragement to our spouse and children ten times more than we criticize them. In other words, for every one criticism, we should have 10 encouraging things to say to them.

Interestingly enough, Dr. John Gottman has studied married couples and he suggests that the best ratio of positive to negative comments is 5 to 1.

According to Harvard Business Review, the highest performing teams in business offer positive comments almost six times more than they offer negative comments.

No matter whether it is family, friends or work, we should be in the business of offering encouraging words.

You can encourage others in several ways:

- You can speak words of encouragement.

- You can send a note, text or e-mail of encouragement.

- You can encourage with a gift or thoughtful item

- Just your presence alone can be an encouragement.

- You can encourage someone by physically helping them.

I have found when I am discouraged; the best way to get out of that "funk" is to encourage someone.   Encouragement is a contagious thing that just seems to multiply and pays huge dividends.   When you are encouraged, you want to encourage others and so on.......

This inspiration for this book came out of a Sunday school lesson I prepared in 2015. I had been asked by our regular teacher if I would consider substituting for him one Sunday and I was very blessed to be asked.

As I prayed about the subject matter for my lesson, I landed upon the theme of encouragement. I had already written a couple of books on encouragement and know how important this subject is for everyone.

Therefore, I started to study characters in the bible and how they were encouraged. I was surprised to see how many of them needed encouragement.

We often see them as "larger than life", but in reality they are just ordinary men and women whom God greatly used to change the world.

I pray as you read this book, you will consider how you can be an encourager to others, and in the process be encouraged yourself.

My hope is that this book will be a blessing to you and your family.

1 Thessalonians 5:11

Therefore encourage one another and build up one another, just as you also are doing.

Romans 15:4-6

For whatever was written in earlier times was written for our instruction, so that through perseverance and the encouragement of the Scriptures we might have hope. Now may the God who gives perseverance and encouragement grant you to be of the same mind with one another according to Christ Jesus, so that with one accord you may with one voice glorify the God and Father of our Lord Jesus Christ.

Hebrews 3:13

But encourage one another day after day, as long as it is still called "Today," so that none of you will be hardened by the deceitfulness of sin.

Even

Moses

Needed
Encouragement

Lessons of Encouragement from the Bible

Moses

A brother to help

Moses is one of the best know characters in the Old Testament. His exploits and deeds are known even to the casual observer of history. From his humble beginnings as an innocent baby in a basket to his rise as a leader of his people, Moses was a mighty man used by God.

As a reminder, here are a few things Moses experienced:

- God speaking from a burning bush
- Confronting Pharaoh - the most powerful man in the world
- Parting the Red Sea
- Water from a Rock
- Manna from Heaven
- Brought forth the 10 Commandments

Moses seems like a larger than life character that could not possibly be real. He seems to be super human, beyond the reach of us mortals. And yet, as you read about his life, you realize he was just a man, and as such, he needed help and encouragement just like the rest of us.

It is interesting to note that Moses was somewhat of a reluctant leader who did not want to speak before Pharaoh. He did not have the self confidence in himself and questioned his abilities. Moses doubted himself, doubts the people will listen to him and doubts anyone will believe him.

Follow this progress as God commands Moses to confront Pharaoh, who, by the way, is the most powerful man in the world at this time (this might also give you "pause" when you really think about it).

Moses is going to make several excuses to God that he hopes will keep him from having to confront Pharaoh.

Moses will pose several questions to God:

- Who am I to do this task?
- Who are you and what should I tell the people who you are?
- What if the people don't believe me?

(As a side note, I think it is somewhat humorous that Moses has these doubts and questions in the first place. Why do I think it is humorous? Because he is talking to a burning bush that is not being consumed, and this is an incredible miracle in and of itself. Yet he has all these doubts. You would think this was enough of a miracle to convince him.)

In Chapter 3 of the book of Exodus, we pick up the story:

God tells Moses to confront Pharaoh and this is Moses response:

Exodus 3:11

But Moses said to God, "Who am I, that I should go to Pharaoh, and that I should bring the sons of Israel out of Egypt?"

Remember that Moses has been away from Egypt for a really long time. He is basically just a shepherd and has been leading a simple life. How will he confront the most powerful man in the world? And more importantly, go back to a country he fled because he had murdered an Egyptian - where certain death awaits him.

God offers the first encouragement to Moses when he doubts himself and his ability to confront Pharaoh.

Exodus 3:12

And He said, "Certainly I will be with you, and this shall be the sign to you that it is I who have sent you: when you have brought the people out of Egypt, you shall worship God at this mountain."

You would think that would enough encouragement for God to say **"I will be with you".** Those are such powerful words of encouragement.

But Moses continues to make excuses. He asks God another question:

Exodus 3:13

Then Moses said to God, "Behold, I am going to the sons of Israel, and I will say to them, 'The God of your fathers has sent me to you.' Now they may say to me, 'What is His name?' What shall I say to them?"

So Moses asks this question and God gives Moses the perfect answer:

Exodus 3:14

God said to Moses, "I AM WHO I AM"; and He said, "Thus you shall say to the sons of Israel, 'I AM has sent me to you.'"

From the different commentaries I have read what God is conveying to Moses about his character in this statement is the following:

- I AM - Self-existent
- I AM - Eternal
- I AM - Unchangeable
- I AM - Faithful and True

This should also have been incredibly encouraging to Moses to know that not only is God with him, but He is faithful and true, never changing and ever present.

God goes on to tell Moses that the elders and people of Israel will listen to him and he needs to go to Pharaoh.

However, Moses has one last excuse up his sleeve:

Exodus 4:1

Then Moses said, "What if they will not believe me or listen to what I say? For they may say, 'The Lord has not appeared to you.'"

Moses again is looking for the reassurance and encouragement before he will go on to do the task set before him. God is good and gracious to be patient with Moses and offer him the encouragement he needs.

God then give Moses the ability to perform two miracles. His staff turns into a snake and his hand become leprous when he puts it in his cloak and then is healed when he puts it back in his cloak. God is loading up Moses with everything he needs to be successful and complete his mission.

Exodus 4:2-8

The Lord said to him, "What is that in your hand?" And he said, "A staff." Then He said, "Throw it on the ground." So he threw it on the ground, and it became a serpent; and Moses fled from it. But the Lord said to Moses, "Stretch out your hand and grasp it by its tail" – so he stretched out his hand and caught it, and it became a staff in his hand – "that they may believe that the Lord, the God of their fathers, the God of Abraham, the God of Isaac, and the God of Jacob, has appeared to you."

The Lord furthermore said to him, "Now put your hand into your bosom." So he put his hand into his bosom, and when he took it out, behold, his hand was leprous like snow. Then He said, "Put your hand into your bosom again." So he put his hand into his bosom again, and when he took it out of his bosom, behold, it was restored like the rest of his flesh. "If they will not believe you or heed the witness of the first sign, they may believe the witness of the last sign.

So Moses has now seen three miracles - the burning bush, the staff to a snake and the leprous hand. As if this is not enough, God gives Moses one more "trump card". The ability to turn water into blood.

Exodus 4:9

(This is God speaking to Moses) - *But if they will not believe even these two signs or heed what you say, then you shall take some water from the Nile and pour it on the dry ground; and the water which you take from the Nile will become blood on the dry ground."*

Therefore, God has now answered all of Moses questions and encouraged him in three specific ways:

1. "I will be with you"
2. "I AM WHO I AM"
3. Gives Moses the ability to perform miracles

This is still not enough for Moses; he starts to whine about his inability to speak and wants out of his mission. God is angry but finally relents and sends Moses brother Aaron onto the scene to help.

Clearly Moses needed someone by his side to offer encouragement and help carry the load.

Aaron turns out to be an incredible companion.   God sends him into the mountains to meet Moses and there Moses tells him everything that God wants them to do.   At this point, they have formed a powerful team.

I love how God is willing to be patient and have this loving, back and forth conversation with Moses and help relieve his fears, offer encouragement and even send someone to be by his side.   We should remember this example as parents or leaders when we need others to perform a difficult task.   They may have doubts and fears and we should be patient and listen.   We should look for solution and offer encouragement and make sure we equip them with all the "tools" they will need to be successful.

Now Moses and Aaron are off to see Pharaoh.

You may have never noticed how closely Moses and Aaron are linked during this incredibly trying time as the nation of Israel tries to break free from their slavery and bondage.   Note that Aaron is right there by the side of Moses through it all.

I had never noticed before all the verses where it says "Moses and Aaron" More than 20 times do you see their names linked together.

Exodus 5:1- Afterward Moses and Aaron went to Pharaoh and said,
Exodus 5:4- Bu the king of Egypt said, "Moses and Aaron ......
Exodus 5:20 -...they met Moses and Aaron as they were waiting ....
Exodus 7:10 - So Moses and Aaron went to Pharaoh.....
Exodus 7:19 - The Lord said to Moses, "Tell Aaron.........
Exodus 7:20 - Moses and Aaron did just as the Lord commanded.
Exodus 7:22 - ....he would not listen to Moses and Aaron...
Exodus 8:5 - Then the Lord said to Moses, "Tell Aaron.........
Exodus 8:8 - Pharaoh summoned Moses and Aaron
Exodus 8:12 - After Moses and Aaron left Pharaoh......
Exodus 8:15 - ....and would not listen to Moses and Aaron;
Exodus 8:16 - Then the Lord said to Moses, "Tell Aaron.........

Exodus 8:25 - Then Pharaoh summoned Moses and Aaron......
Exodus 9:8 - Then the Lord said to Moses and Aaron.........
Exodus 9:27 - Then Pharaoh summoned Moses and Aaron......
Exodus 10:3 - So Moses and Aaron went to Pharaoh.....
Exodus 10:8 - Then Moses and Aaron were brought back to Pharaoh.
Exodus 10:11 -....... Then Moses and Aaron were driven out.........
Exodus 10:16 - Pharaoh quickly summoned Moses and Aaron.....
Exodus 11:10 - Moses and Aaron performed all these wonders....
Exodus 12:1 - The Lord said to Moses and Aaron in Egypt,
Exodus 12:31 - ... Pharaoh summoned Moses and Aaron...
Exodus 12:43- The Lord said to Moses and Aaron
Exodus 12:43-...... had commanded Moses and Aaron

Wow, from chapters 4-12 in the book of Exodus, almost every time you
see the name of Moses you see Aarons name as well.   No doubt this
was a great encouragement to Moses.   You see, Moses was just a
normal man that God chose to use in extraordinary ways.

  In the same way you and I need others to be our "Aaron" and come
beside us and at other times, we need to become "Aaron" to others and
be an encourager to them.   In these examples, Aaron is the mouth
piece and companion for Moses.

So Moses is able to accomplish the mission set before him because God
is able to adequately encourage him along the way.

  In this next example you will see how Aaron was able to offer
encouragement in a very different way.

In the time that Moses had lead the people out of Egypt, there was
much groaning and moaning as they confronted different obstacles.
God parted the Red Sea, brought them manna from heaven and water
from a rock.   Now they must confront an enemy in battle.

We are introduced to Joshua at this juncture of the story and Joshua is
now commanded to go and fight the Amalekites   Moses promised
victory as long as he held the staff of God in his hands.

Here is where Aaron and Hur are able to offer physical encouragement
to Moses.   Read the following verses:

Exodus 17:8-13

*Then Amalek came and fought against Israel at Rephidim. So Moses said to Joshua, "Choose men for us and go out, fight against Amalek. Tomorrow I will station myself on the top of the hill with the staff of God in my hand." Joshua did as Moses told him, and fought against Amalek; and Moses, Aaron, and Hur went up to the top of the hill. So it came about when Moses held his hand up, that Israel prevailed, and when he let his hand down, Amalek prevailed. **But Moses' hands were heavy. Then they took a stone and put it under him, and he sat on it; and Aaron and Hur supported his hands, one on one side and one on the other.** Thus his hands were steady until the sun set. So Joshua overwhelmed Amalek and his people with the edge of the sword.*

You see, sometimes we just need to come alongside someone and help them physically to encourage them. In this case, they were literally holding Moses hands up. Moses needed these men to come alongside him to help complete the task.

We cannot and should not expect our leaders to do all the work themselves. Leaders need help and encouragement as much as anybody else.

Try to imagine who was encouraged that day.

1. The Israelites watching the battle would have been so encouraged to see their leader on the hill overlooking the battle and Joshua in the valley fighting for them.
2. Joshua would have been encouraged to know his leaders were doing everything in their power to help him be successful
3. Moses would have been encouraged by the love and devotion of these men to help him.
4. Aaron and Hur would have been encouraged by seeing the positive impact of their intervention and help.

Encouragement pays big dividends for everyone involved. It has ripple effects that you may not even see in your life time. Later in the book you will see how Moses encourages Joshua as he takes the reins as the new leader of the nation of Israel.

Worksheet

Take time to answer the questions, pray and reflect on what you just read in this chapter and how you might apply the learning to your life.

List all of the leaders in your life (work, home church, social, etc) :

1.
2.
3.
4.
5.
6.
7.
8.
9.
10.

Do any of these leaders need encouragement? If you don't know, how could you find out (in a nonthreatening or intrusive way).

How can you use your time, talents and treasures to encourage your leader?

At a minimum, take the time now to pray for your leaders and add them to your prayer journal.

Beggar
A hand up

Imagine for a moment that you had been crippled from birth. In ancient times you would have been cursed and reviled.   Many would have thought that either you or your parents must have been sinners and were only getting what you deserved.

There were no social programs or government to help you.   Your only option was to beg.

To be a beggar was demeaning and lowly.

You would be completely dependent on the kindness and goodness of others each and every day. Someone would have to take you to a location to beg and then you would have to humiliate yourself and ask others for a gift.

I have to believe that you would have no self-esteem and it would be difficult to even look others in the eye.

I have seen people on the side of the road here in Atlanta with signs begging for food or money and rarely do I see them making meaningful eye contact. They are almost always downcast, ashamed of the position they are in.

If anyone needed encouragement, it would be a beggar and someone who had been a disabled their entire life.

Peter and John are minding their own business one day as they headed to the temple to pray. See how Peter and John offer a "hand up" to someone who is usually ignored by society.

Acts 3:1-10

Now Peter and John were going up to the temple at the ninth hour, the hour of prayer. And a man who had been lame from his mother's womb was being carried along, whom they used to set down every day at the gate of the temple which is called Beautiful, in order to beg alms of those who were entering the temple. When he saw Peter and John about to go into the temple, he began asking to receive alms. But Peter, along with John, fixed his gaze on him and said, "Look at us!" And he began to give them his attention, expecting to receive something from them.
But Peter said, "I do not possess silver and gold, but what I do have I give to you: In the name of Jesus Christ the Nazarene – walk!" **And seizing him by the right hand**, *he raised him up; and immediately his feet and his ankles were strengthened. With a leap he stood upright and began to walk; and he entered the temple with them, walking and leaping and praising God. And all the people saw him walking and praising God; and they were taking note of him as being the one who used to sit at the Beautiful Gate of the temple to beg alms, and they were filled with wonder and amazement at what had happened to him.*

They reached down to him at his level! How many of us are willing to reach down to someone who is in this condition? They saw his need and offered him what he really needed. Not money, but healing!

What did the man do after that? He leaped for joy and praised God. He had been healed. We learn later in chapter 4 that the man was over 40 years old and obviously well known to many of the people in Jerusalem.   Not only was this man encouraged, but many people heard the story and were encouraged.

Encouragement is contagious. It spreads easily when proclaimed. When you encourage one person you are really starting a chain reaction no less powerful than splitting an atom.   Encouragement has a multiplier effect that cannot easily be stopped or contained.

Commit today to be a person of encouragement. Look for opportunities to encourage others, especially someone you don't necessarily know.   See how God can use your gift of encouragement to start a chain reaction.

<u>Worksheet</u>

Take time to answer the questions, pray and reflect on what you just read in this chapter and how you might apply the learning to your life.

Do you know someone who "needs a hand up"?

How can you personally interject encouragement into their life?

Who can you enlist to help you offer encouragement to this individual or family?

What will it "cost" you to offer the encouragement (in terms of time, talent and treasures)?

What is their worldly real need?   What is their spiritual need?

Ruth

A loyal daughter in-law

You are a mother and your family is hungry! There is famine in the land. What are you to do? You must have food to feed your family. The sensible thing to do is move to where you can find food.

The hard part is leaving family, friends and the familiar behind. You are stepping out on faith and into the unknown. You follow your husband and load up your sons to take them to a more promising future.

However, more tragedy strikes.

Your husband dies, and you are left with two sons in a strange land. You are now a widow, but at least you still have your sons to help you through this difficult time. Your sons marry and you live in this strange land for 10 years.

But then more tragedy strikes.

Both of your boys die. You are widow in a strange land, with only your daughter in-laws to comfort you.

In ancient time, to be a widow was tantamount to being in poverty.

This is the situation that Naomi found herself while in the land of Moab. I cannot begin to image her grief and sorrow. Clearly she was in the depths of despair and mourning. Her thoughts turned to home and any family she might have there in the land of Judah.

She had come to the land of Moab married with two sons and now she would return a poor widow with no sons (meaning no one to care for her).

How discouraged was Naomi?

She was so discouraged that she asked that her name be changed from Naomi (which means pleasant) to Mara (which means bitter).

In spite of her great difficulty, Naomi was a thoughtful mother in-law.

She did not want to be a burden to Orpah and Ruth (her daughters in law) and begged them to go home to their own mothers and family. In this way she knew they might have a good chance to marry again, and at a minimum, be surrounded by their family members.

She wanted them to move on with their lives and find new husbands and homes. It was an unbelievably unselfish act.

We then find what I believe is one of the most powerful verses in the bible when it comes to encouragement and loyalty. Her daughter in-law Ruth is having nothing to do with this plan. See what she says to Naomi:

Ruth 1:16-17

But Ruth said, "Do not urge me to leave you or turn back from following you; for where you go, I will go, and where you lodge, I will lodge. Your people shall be my people, and your God, my God. Where you die, I will die, and there I will be buried. Thus may the Lord do to me, and worse, if anything but death parts you and me."

This is such a powerful statement of encouragement that many people include it in their marriage vows.

What an incredible thing for Naomi's to hear at this lowest point in her life. It would have been very easy for Ruth to take the easy way out, but she chose love and loyalty over the easy and convenient. What an unbelievably positive example for all of us!

Naomi now had a loyal companion to carry her burden, to travel with, to talk to and share fond memories. While I am sure Naomi was still in grief and sorrow, she must have also been greatly encouraged by the loyalty and love of Ruth.

Where does all of this end?   The story of Ruth is such a beautiful story of continuing encouragement.

Boaz (a relative of Naomi's late husband) offers food, water and shelter to Ruth (who is a foreigner in the land).   He does so, because he has heard the story of Ruth and how well she treated Naomi.   You see, encouragement never stops with just the person you encourage.   You also reap what you sew.

Can you image how encouraged Ruth was by the kindness and generosity of Boaz?

Naomi then offers really good advice and counsel to Ruth in terms of here relationship and interactions with Boaz. Naomi has Ruth's best interest in mind and wants her to have a fruitful and successful life. Naomi knows that she is an "old" widow and would probably not be married again, but she did not hold back in helping Ruth.

Ruth goes on to marry Boaz and he turns out to be kind, loving and compassionate.

They have a son named Obed, who has a son named Jesse, who has a son named David. Yes that David. King David. A direct descendant of Jesus!

What started in sorrow and grief ends with a King - THE KING!

We can never see end-to-end in any situation. Only God knows the beginning and the end.

When you have the opportunity this week, look for ways to encourage others.   You never know where that encouragement will "end".

 Be encouraged and encourage others.

Worksheet

Take time to answer the questions, pray and reflect on what you just read in this chapter and how you might apply the learning to your life.

Does your church have a specific ministry to the widows? If so, how can you help support that ministry? If not, how can you find widows to encourage in your church?

Take time to pray for the widows in your church and community.

Is there a widow in your life you need to encourage (mother, aunt, sister, grandmother). See verse below:

1 Timothy 5:3-4

Honor widows who are widows indeed; but if any widow has children or grandchildren, they must first learn to practice piety in regard to their own family and to make some return to their parents; for this is acceptable in the sight of God.

Adam

A suitable helper

In the beginning, God created this world and he created Adam as the first human.   It was on the sixth day after he had created light, sky, land, seas, sun, moon and stars and all of the animals.

Genesis 1:27 -

So God created man in his own image, in the image of God he created him;

God created an amazing place for Adam to dwell and live.   The Garden of Eden would provide all of his needs as well as offer a place of peace and rest.

However, God recognized that Adam would need companionship as well for fellowship and encouragement.

Genesis 2:18

Then the Lord God said, "It is not good for the man to be alone; I will make him a helper suitable for him."

He created all of the animals and brought them to Adam to name.   It must have been amazing and fascinating for Adam to see all of these beasts.   Some would have been beautiful and cuddly (like a dog or rabbit), others would be strong and powerful (like a lion) and still others would have been course and ugly (like a warthog).   Yet none of these animals could be a "suitable helper" for Adam. None could offer encouragement and help him with the trials and tribulations of life.

Genesis 2:20-22

......but for Adam there was not found a helper suitable for him. So the Lord God caused a deep sleep to fall upon the man, and he slept; then He took one of his ribs and closed up the flesh at that place. The Lord God fashioned into a woman the rib which He had taken from the man, and brought her to the man.

God knew that Adam would need someone by his side to offer encouragement and help.

Eve could speak her words of encouragement; she could be by his side when he felt like a failure or simply hold him when words were not necessary.

In the same way Adam could offer encouragement and comfort to Eve.

Genesis 2:24

For this reason a man shall leave his father and his mother, and be joined to his wife; and they shall become one flesh.

When you are married you become "one" with your spouse. This means that when you are encouraged, they will be encouraged. When you are discouraged, they will be discouraged. There is no way to separate "one flesh" (without great pain and suffering and even then, it will never be as it was before).

So how can you encourage your bride?

- Recognize that she is a gift from God and be thankful
- Know she is more precious than jewels and treat her as such
- Know that you will find favor with God and share that with her
- Rejoice in your relationship even when you grow old
- Do not treat her harshly
- Always be faithful to your bride
- You can lift her up when she falls
- Live with her in an understanding way
- Love her as Christ loves the church
- Love her as you love yourself

Read the following verses and think about your relationship with your bride.

Proverbs 12:4

An excellent wife is the crown of her husband,

Proverbs 18:22

He who finds a wife finds a good thing
And obtains favor from the Lord.

Proverbs 19:14

House and wealth are an inheritance from fathers,
But a prudent wife is from the Lord.

Proverbs 31:10

An excellent wife, who can find?
For her worth is far above jewels.

Proverbs 5:18-19

Let your fountain be blessed,
And rejoice in the wife of your youth.
As a loving hind and a graceful doe,
Let her breasts satisfy you at all times;
Be exhilarated always with her love.

Colossians 3:19

Husbands, love your wives and do not be embittered against them.

1 Peter 3:7

You husbands in the same way live with your wives in an understanding way, as with someone weaker, since she is a woman; and show her honor as a fellow heir of the grace of life, so that your prayers will not be hindered.

Hebrews 13:4

Marriage is to be held in honor among all, and the marriage bed is to be undefiled; for fornicators and adulterers God will judge.

Ephesians 5:25-33

Husbands, love your wives, just as Christ also loved the church and gave Himself up for her, so that He might sanctify her, having cleansed her by the washing of water with the word, that He might present to Himself the church in all her glory, having no spot or wrinkle or any such thing; but that she would be holy and blameless. So husbands ought also to love their own wives as their own bodies. He who loves his own wife loves himself; 29 for no one ever hated his own flesh, but nourishes and cherishes it, just as Christ also does the church, because we are members of His body. For this reason a man shall leave his father and mother and shall be joined to his wife, and the two shall become one flesh. This mystery is great; but I am speaking with reference to Christ and the church. 33 Nevertheless, each individual among you also is to love his own wife even as himself, and the wife must see to it that she respects her husband.

Ecclesiastes 4:9-11

Two are better than one because they have a good return for their labor. For if either of them falls, the one will lift up his companion. But woe to the one who falls when there is not another to lift him up. Furthermore, if two lie down together they keep warm, but how can one be warm alone?

Even from the beginning of time, God knew that we would need encouragement and help. You were created for a greater purpose than to just fulfil your own needs and desires. You can be that encourager who makes a difference today.

The choice is yours. I pray you would choose to be an encourager.

Worksheet

Take time to answer the questions, pray and reflect on what you just read in this chapter and how you might apply the learning to your life.

Do you need to be encouraged today in regards to your marriage? Why?

Does your spouse need encouragement? What can you do right now to encourage them?

What are your spouses "Love Language"? If you don't know, find out! There is a great book by Gary Chapman the list the five love languages and by using them you can encourage your spouse greatly. Here are the five love languages:

- Gifts

- Quality Time

- Words of Affirmation,

- Acts of Service

- Physical Touch

When you learn the love language of your spouse and put that into practical use, you will be amazed at the way this can transform your relationship. I encourage you to read the book or at a minimum go to the website and learn more about the love languages.

Joseph

A good brother

There are several "Josephs" in the bible.

- There is Jesus earthly father -Joseph,
- There is Joseph in the New Testament - known as Barnabas - we will get to him later
- And there is also Joseph of Arimathia who helped to bury Jesus after his crucifixion.

This story is about Joseph of the Old Testament. This is the Joseph who had the coat of many colors and was hated by his brothers. . He was a favored son of his Father and was treated with more love and kindness - this caused his brothers to despise him.

What is most interesting about this Joseph is that for most of his early life he was in desperate need of encouragement.

Without retelling his entire store in detail, here is brief chronology of what happened early in Joseph's life: (told in Genesis 37-50)

- He is favored by his father (he was the youngest son at that time)
- His brothers hated him and conspired to kill him - not a good start
- Instead of killing Joseph his brothers sold him into slavery - He is 17 years old.
- He becomes a slave in Potiphar's house in Egypt
- Things go from bad to worse as Potiphar's wife falsely accuses him of molesting her
- Joseph is thrown in jail

- Joseph helps the chief cupbearer by interpreting a dream and asks for his help to get out of jail, but two years pass before he is remembered.

However, God is good and gracious to Joseph through all of this turmoil. Note that twice the bible tells us that "The Lord was with Joseph".

Genesis 39:2

The Lord was with Joseph, so he became a successful man. And he was in the house of his master, the Egyptian.

Genesis 39:21

But the Lord was with Joseph and extended kindness to him, and gave him favor in the sight of the chief jailer.

Joseph was 17 when he entered slavery and prison and did not get out of this situation until he was 30 years old! He spent 13 years in this situation.

How would you feel?

Might you be bitter, frustrated, and angry?

How would you feel towards your brothers? The word that comes to my mind is hatred!

However God has a new plan and the next years are a different story for Joseph:

- Pharaoh (the most powerful man in the world), makes Joseph second in command. He is now running the entire country
- Pharaoh gives him a new name - Zaphenath-Paneah
- Pharaoh gives him the daughter of a high official to marry
- He has two sons
- No one in the kingdom is greater than him other than Pharaoh

Joseph is now clearly blessed and a man in power and control.

Now begin the seven years of plenty followed by seven years of famine. Joseph had interpreted Pharaohs dream that predicted what would happen and this is why he was placed in charge of the country to store up grain for the seven years of famine.

Enter Joseph's brothers again. This time, they are coming to Egypt to purchase grain because they are starving and in famine as well.

Joseph recognizes his brothers, but they do not recognize him. They had sold him into slavery when he was 17 and now he was 37. It had been more than 20 years since they had reported him dead to their father.

Joseph can now exact his revenge! He is "large and in charge".

However, Joseph chooses a different path instead.

He put his brothers through several twists and turns and clearly causes them some anxiety and frustration, but it seems more playful than vengeance.

Finally after some time passes he reveals himself to his brothers. Remember they think he is dead and are about to be very surprised to find that the second most powerful man in Egypt is their brother.

How did his brothers react?

Genesis 45:3

Then Joseph said to his brothers, "I am Joseph! Is my father still alive?" But his brothers could not answer him, for they were dismayed (terrified) at his presence.

We all know why they were terrified. They knew now that their lives were forfeit and that they were basically dead meat!!!

Now here comes the encouragement. I cannot help but be deeply moved every time I read this passage. Joseph had every right to exact revenge and payback, but he did not! See what he says:

Genesis 45:4-11

Then Joseph said to his brothers, "Please come closer to me." And they came closer. And he said, "I am your brother Joseph, whom you sold into Egypt. Now do not be grieved or angry with yourselves, because you sold me here, for God sent me before you to preserve life. For the famine has been in the land these two years, and there are still five years in which there will be neither plowing nor harvesting. God sent me before you to preserve for you a remnant in the earth, and to keep you alive by a great deliverance. Now, therefore, it was not you who sent me here, but God; and He has made me a father to Pharaoh and lord of all his household and ruler over all the land of Egypt. Hurry and go up to my father, and say to him, 'Thus says your son Joseph, "God has made me lord of all Egypt; come down to me, do not delay. You shall live in the land of Goshen, and you shall be near me, you and your children and your children's children and your flocks and your herds and all that you have. There I will also provide for you, for there are still five years of famine to come, and you and your household and all that you have would be impoverished."'

Wow! Not only does he forgive them, but he is going to provide for their needs and the needs of their family. Do you think they were encouraged (and relieved). Their hearts must have soared that day.

They deserved death and instead were given life! And not only life, but an abundant life in this time of this great famine.

They were shown both mercy and grace by their brother.

Mercy - not getting what we do deserve

Grace - getting what we do not deserve

Think about how this closely this mirrors the mercy and grace we receive from God! We are all sinners deserving hell and death and yet through Christ Jesus and his death, burial and resurrection we receive God's mercy and grace when we trust Him as our Lord and Savior!

Now what is great is that the story of Joseph is that it just gets better!

Another 17 year pass and now Joseph is 54 years old. His beloved father has just passed away and his brothers fear for their lives again. They felt that the only reason they were still alive was because of their father and his relationship with Joseph.

They threw themselves at Josephs feet and said "we are your slaves"

What Joseph does next is incredible!

Genesis 50:19-21

But Joseph said to them, "Do not be afraid, for am I in God's place? As for you, you meant evil against me, but God meant it for good in order to bring about this present result, to preserve many people alive. So therefore, do not be afraid; I will provide for you and your little ones." So he comforted them and spoke kindly to them.

Final encouragement where none is expected! From the worlds perspective he had every right to be bitter and angry. He had every right to exact vengeance and then some! Instead he chose mercy, grace and encouragement.

Would you be able to offer encouragement to someone who has done you a great harm?

It is a question I ask myself as I write this chapter. I don't think I could without the grace of God in my life.

Do you know God's grace and mercy? Follow the "Romans Road" and see how God has laid out his plan of salvation for your life:

Romans Road

Romans 3:23 – *for all have sinned and fall short of the glory of God.*

We must all realize that we are sinners and that we need forgiveness. We are not worthy of God's grace.

Romans 6:23– *For the wages of sin is death, but the gift of God is eternal life in Christ Jesus our Lord.*

If we remain sinners, we will die. However, if we accept Jesus as our Lord and Savior, and repent of our sins, we will have eternal life

Romans 5:8 – *But God demonstrates His own love toward us, in that while we were still sinners, Christ died for us.*

Through Jesus, God gave us a way to be saved from our sins. God showed us His love by giving us the potential for life through the death of His Son, Jesus Christ.

Romans 10:9-10 – *that if you confess with your mouth the Lord Jesus and believe in your heart that God has raised Him from the dead, you will be saved. For with the heart one believes unto righteousness, and with the mouth confession is made unto salvation*

Just confess that Jesus Christ is Lord and believe in your heart that God raised Him from the dead and you will be saved!

Romans 10:13 – *For "whoever calls on the name of the LORD shall be saved."*

There are no religious formulas or rituals -- Call upon the name of the Lord and you will be saved!

Romans 10:17– *So then faith comes by hearing, and hearing by the word of God.*

God's plan of salvation is simple and free.   There is nothing you can do to "earn" it.   You only need to believe and confess.

I followed this path of salvation in many years ago as a teenager and my life has never been the same. I pray you will follow this path to God's love and forgiveness.

Read the entire story of Joseph in Genesis 37 - 50.   It is an incredibly inspiring story and I have not done it justice in these few pages.

Worksheet

Take time to answer the questions, pray and reflect on what you just read in this chapter and how you might apply the learning to your life.

Do you have a sibling that you need to encourage today?

Do any of you siblings have areas where they struggle and you can help and come alongside them?

Is there someone who is "close as a brother" that you need to encourage today?

Joshua

Next in Line

Have you ever been the one waiting in the wings for your time on the main stage? You have watched your mentor and leader for years and soon it will be your turn to be the leader. That can be very intimidating for anyone to handle. There will be doubts and fears and perhaps thoughts of inadequacy.

The leader in this case is Moses. Moses has been a great leader and God has used him in a miraculous way to lead the people of Israel out of Egypt. Moses has taken them across the Red Sea and into the wilderness for 40 years. He has been their one constant since they have left their slavery and oppression. A whole generation has grown up in the wilderness and only knows the stories of Egypt that have been passed down from their elders.

Moses is a great leader and realizes that his time has passed and God will not allow him to cross over into the Promised Land. Therefore, he wants to encourage the people before they continue their journey.

Deuteronomy 31:6

Be strong and courageous, do not be afraid or tremble at them, for the Lord your God is the one who goes with you. He will not fail you or forsake you."

These are powerful words that must have filled the people's hearts with hope and encouragement.

Moses gives then three distinct points that should help them to be strong and courageous. He tells the people:

1. God will go with you
2. God will not fail you (God is faithful) some translations say that God will not leave you
3. God will not forsake you

As you read these words think about others who may be heading into the "Wilderness" and how you can encourage them today. What are some "Wilderness" areas that someone may be heading into? Here are a few that give people some "pause":

- New job
- Marriage
- Birth of a child
- Loss of loved one
- Moving to a new city or country
- A physical or mental challenge

These "wilderness" areas can be scary because they are new territory that has never been tread before. However, those same words that Moses spoke to the nation of Israel are true for you today. In addition we have some additional powerful scripture to encourage us as we head into the "wilderness". Consider these two verses:

Romans 8:31

What then shall we say to these things? If God is for us, who is against us?

1 John 4:4

You are from God, little children, and have overcome them; because greater is He who is in you than he who is in the world.

These are great verses to memorize and have ready for instant recall. They have been a great comfort to me in times of trouble and distress.

PASSING THE TORCH

They say that it is lonely at the top because everyone is looking at you and you have no one to confide in and talk to. Joshua is about to find out.

All this time Joshua has been sitting in crowd watching and learning from this great leader and now it will soon be his turn to lead.

Moses is not done, he knows that he must have a discussion with Joshua and pass the torch. He knows how difficult it is to be a leader and how lonely and challenging the task will be for Joshua. Moses knows this and wants to offer some personal words of encouragement to Joshua as he gets ready to take the reins.

Deuteronomy 31:7-8

*Then Moses called to Joshua and said to him in the sight of all Israel, "**Be strong and courageous,** for you shall go with this people into the land which the Lord has sworn to their fathers to give them, and you shall give it to them as an inheritance. The Lord is the one who goes ahead of you; He will be with you. He will not fail you or forsake you. Do not fear or be dismayed."*

Moses offers Joshua the same encouragement that he offered the nation of Israel:

> 1. God will go with you
> 2. God will not fail you (God is faithful) some translations say that God will not leave you
> 3. God will not forsake you

Like any good leader, Moses knows that you need to offer the same message over and over again so that it will sink in and people will take it to heart.

Moses has done his job and is finishing well. He has encouraged Joshua and is now ready to let him be the new leader.

Moses passes away and now reality of leadership hits Joshua full force. He is "the man". He must now lead.

Then God steps in and starts Joshua on his journey with some very strong encouragement.

In the next passage you will see that three times God says to Joshua:

"BE STRONG AND COURAGEOUS"

"BE STRONG AND COURAGEOUS"

"BE STRONG AND COURAGEOUS"

God knows what lies ahead for Joshua and he is preparing him for leaderships and the challenge he will face.

God then tells Joshua two key things:

1. "I will never leave you nor forsake you"
2. "... the Lord your God will be with you wherever you go"

On the first item, God is reminding Joshua what Moses had already told him earlier. Moses had used these exact same words to describe how God would treat Joshua.

On the second item, it is God's way to reminding Joshua that he will never be alone in his leadership. God was going to be with him and Joshua would need to learn how to lean into God in times of trouble and doubt.

Read the verses below and be encouraged and know that we serve a great God who is always looking for ways to encourage his children.

(note the emphasis in the passage has been added by me)

This is God speaking to Joshua:

Joshua 1:5-9

..."*No man will be able to stand before you all the days of your life. Just as I have been with Moses, I will be with you; I will not fail you or forsake you. **Be strong and courageous**, for you shall give this people possession of the land which I swore to their fathers to give them. **Only be strong and very courageous**; be careful to do according to all the law which Moses My servant commanded you; do not turn from it to the right or to the left, so that you may have success wherever you go. This book of the law shall not depart from your mouth, but you shall meditate on it day and night, so that you may be careful to do according to all that is written in it; for then you will make your way prosperous, and then you will have success. Have I not commanded you? **Be strong and courageous**! Do not tremble or be dismayed, for the Lord your God is with you wherever you go.*"

We are all leaders in one way or another. Consider these words and think about how you need to constantly be offering words of encouragement to those who are following you. By offering the same message over and over again, you will let them know you are consistent in your words and deeds and that they can trust you.

If a consistent message from God is good enough for Joshua, it is good enough for you and I today.

What a glorious and wonderful God we serve! To God be the glory.

Be encouraged.

Worksheet

Take time to answer the questions, pray and reflect on what you just read in this chapter and how you might apply the learning to your life.

Is there a young leader in your church who could use some encouragement today?

Are you in the "Wilderness" or heading into the "Wilderness"?   Pray that God will give you wisdom and discernment to guide you along the right path.

Do you know someone who is in the "Wilderness" that you can use encourage today?   Reach out to them now with a kind word.   At a minimum, lift them up in prayer.

Pray for the leaders of you church and congregation and look for ways to encourage them in all areas of their life:

- Relational
- Financial
- Physical
- Mental
- Spiritual
- Occupational

Job
A Friend in Need

Life is just wonderful!. You have a bunch of stuff you can check off your list:

- ✓ You have an incredible wife
- ✓ Wonderful children
- ✓ Business is doing very well
- ✓ You have good health
- ✓ Your relationship with God is really good.

What could possibly go wrong?

Most people would say you "had it made"!

Then your world gets turned upside down.

- You lose your business and your employees are slaughtered
- All of your children are killed
- Your health declines rapidly
- Your relationship with your wife is fragile.

Do you think you might be in need of a little encouragement?

What would be your frame of mind at this time? I have to believe that I would be a mess. I would probably be angry, sad, depressed and hurt. I know I would need encouragement.

This is where Job has found himself. His story is one that few of us could endure.

We pick up the story in the book of Job where he is described as blameless and upright. He has 10 children, 10,000 + animals and a multitude of servants. In other words, he is rich and blessed.

Then in a series of tests, he loses everything.

First raiders come and steal all of his animals, and then all of his children are killed by a powerful storm. Yet he does not sin or blame God.

In fact, see how he reacts to the disaster, it is really quite incredible!

Job 1:20-22

Then Job arose and tore his robe and shaved his head, and he fell to the ground and worshiped. He said,

"Naked I came from my mother's womb,
And naked I shall return there.
The Lord gave and the Lord has taken away.
Blessed be the name of the Lord."

Through all this Job did not sin nor did he blame God.

The bible says that he worshiped God! What a powerful testimony to his life and relationship with God.

In the next phase of tests his health is taken from him. He is struck for head to sole, with boils.

I have been unfortunate enough to have a boil or two in my life time. They are **VERY** painful and debilitating. They do not heal quickly and also scar the skin very badly after they heal. I cannot imagine my entire body covered by boils. The pain and misery must have been completely overwhelming.

At a time like this, I would be looking to my best friend to comfort and encourage me, to help me and stand by my side. My best friend is my Bride and I know she would be there for me. However in the case of Job, his wife was just the opposite. She actually piled on and discouraged the man. See her reaction:

Job 2:9

Then his wife said to him, "Do you still hold fast your integrity? Curse God and die!"

Not exactly the words you want to hear at this time. "Curse God and Die"! Ouch!!

All Job had left at this time was his integrity. Everything else had been taken from him.

(I always have to remind myself that she has lost all her children, wealth and possessions and now her husband is in great physical pain. She is obviously hurting as well and could use encouragement herself. It is difficult to offer encouragement when you are in the valley of despair).

Sometimes, when people are hurting, we do not need to say anything to encourage them. In fact, saying anything at all just might be the wrong thing and actually discourage them. In the case of Job he had three really good friends who came along to encourage him.

These three guys had heard that Job was having a difficult time and agreed that they should go and see him and comfort him.

What great friends! We all need friends like this in our life and more importantly, we need to be a friend like this.

Job 2:11

Now when Job's three friends heard of all this adversity that had come upon him, they came each one from his own place, Eliphaz the Temanite, Bildad the Shuhite and Zophar the Naamathite; and they made an appointment together to come to sympathize with him and comfort him.

However, when they see him, they don't even recognize their friend. They begin to cry and weep for their friend. The can see he is in physical pain, but his emotional pain is probably evident as well.

They don't say a word for 7 days! They just stick close to him and are there for him as only a friend can be. I can only imagine (since it does not say in the bible), that they ministered to his needs and took care of their friend.

You may have a time in your life when you have a close friend or family member who is hurting and just needs you close by for comfort. There is no need to talk or exchange words. You just need to be there. Silence is golden!

Final Word

In the end, Job's friends mess up and start talking! They start trying to solve the problem as they see it, but are not real helpful. It would have been better to keep their mouths shut!

Remember, you can encourage just by your presence. If you don't have something encouraging to say in this type of circumstance, then don't say anything at all. Just be there in silence.

Worksheet

Take time to answer the questions, pray and reflect on what you just read in this chapter and how you might apply the learning to your life.

Do you have a friend who is hurting and needs you by their side?

How can you encourage them without saying a thing?

Take time right now to pray for them.

Also, remember their family members who may also be hurting and need encouragement as well.

Gideon

Reassurance - seeing is believing

All of us have doubts.

What if you were considered the smallest, weakest and least amongst your friends and family?   Might you have a bit of a self-confidence issue?

If you had an important task and opportunity presented to you, might you have some doubts and questions?   Would you need some reassurance and encouragement to complete the task?

Gideon sure did!

The nation of Israel had been handed over to their enemies because of their sinfulness.   For seven years they suffered and cried out to God for deliverance from their enemies.

God was going to deliver them, but not in the way they were thinking. He was going to choose someone from among them to lead the way - someone they themselves would not have chosen.

God chooses Gideon.

Gideon is minding his own business and threshing some wheat.   He is a person in the background and this is probably where he prefers to be most of the time. He considers himself small and weak and not one to look for trouble.

God sends an angel to speak to Gideon and he greets him with unusual words that he has never heard before:

Judges 6:12

The angel of the Lord appeared to him (Gideon) *and said to him, "The Lord is with you, O valiant* (or mighty) *warrior."*

Mighty warrior? Ha!   I bet Gideon wanted to laugh.

Gideon proceeds to have an interesting discussion with the angel of God, in which it appears that he really does not want to take up the mantle of "mighty warrior" or lead the people out of the hands of their enemy.

Gideon questions himself - "my clan is the weakest and I am the least of my family"

Judges 6:15

He (Gideon) *said to Him, "O Lord, how shall I deliver Israel? Behold, my family is the least in Manasseh, and I am the youngest in my father's house."*

Gideon needs reassurance that this is really God and really the path he needs to go down.

The angel tells him "I will be with you, and you will strike down all the Midianites".

Judges 6:16

But the Lord said to him, "Surely I will be with you, and you shall defeat Midian as one man."

What powerful words of encouragement. "I will be with you"

But this is not enough for Gideon, he goes on to ask God to perform a couple of miracles so that he can be really sure that God is with him. For Gideon, "seeing is believing". Words are ok, but he wants to see God in action before he is willing to commit.

Judges 6:36-40

Then Gideon said to God, "If You will deliver Israel through me, as You have spoken, behold, I will put a fleece of wool on the threshing floor. If there is dew on the fleece only, and it is dry on all the ground, then I will know that You will deliver Israel through me, as You have spoken." And it was so. When he arose early the next morning and squeezed the fleece, he drained the dew from the fleece, a bowl full of water.

Then Gideon said to God, "Do not let Your anger burn against me that I may speak once more; please let me make a test once more with the fleece, let it now be dry only on the fleece, and let there be dew on all the ground." God did so that night; for it was dry only on the fleece, and dew was on all the ground.

Gideon needed this reassurance and encouragement. He was about to go into battle and wanted to be sure. However, even with these miracles, Gideon is going to need one more miracle before the battle.

Gideon forms his army and is ready with 32,000 warriors. This is a nice large group of men to go to battle with and defeat their enemy.

However, God has another plan and reduces Gideon's ranks of men from 32,000 to 300! I am pretty sure that I would have my own doubts and would need some encouragement at that point.

God steps in again with one last miracle before the battle. He wakes up Gideon and has a message for him.

Judges 7:10-15

But if you are afraid to go down, go with Purah your servant down to the camp, and you will hear what they say; and afterward your hands will be strengthened that you may go down against the camp." So he went with Purah his servant down to the outposts of the army that was in the camp. Now the Midianites and the Amalekites and all the sons of the east were lying in the valley as numerous as locusts; and their camels were without number, as numerous as the sand on the seashore. When Gideon came, behold, a man was relating a dream to his friend. And he said, "Behold, I had a dream; a loaf of barley bread was tumbling into the camp of Midian, and it came to the tent and struck it so that it fell, and turned it upside down so that the tent lay flat." 14 His friend replied, "This is nothing less than the sword of Gideon the son of Joash, a man of Israel; God has given Midian and all the camp into his hand."

When Gideon heard the account of the dream and its interpretation, he bowed in worship. He returned to the camp of Israel and said, "Arise, for the Lord has given the camp of Midian into your hands."

God knows the heart of Gideon and knows that he needs encouragement and reassurance. God has asked Gideon to perform what would appears to be an impossible task, and God is not about to send him on his way without this encouragement.

We all need reassurance, especially before an important task. If you are a parent, think about how you can encourage you children and reassure them when they have doubts and fears. You might have to offer this encouragement multiple times, but do not grow weary with offering the encouragement or think that it is not important.

If God can go to such great lengths to encourage Gideon, then we should do the same as parents, spouses and friends. Look for opportunities to encourage your loved ones and those around you.

Worksheet

Take time to answer the questions, pray and reflect on what you just read in this chapter and how you might apply the learning to your life.

Do you face a difficult task that seems impossible?

- **Pray that God would give you courage**

- **Pray the God would send people your way to encourage you**

- **Look for ways to encourage others, even as you struggle**

- **When you don't know what to do, do what you know to do - that is - fast, pray, worship, study, praise and be in fellowship with other believers**

David

Finding a soul mate

Who was David really? He was the youngest son of Jesse and not even big enough to be considered worthy of doing anything other than being a shepherd.   However, God does not look at the outward appearance of David, but considers his heart and knows that he will be the next King of Israel.

God has rejected King Saul as the leader of Israel and has sent the prophet Samuel to anoint the next King.   Samuel goes to see Jesse and all of his oldest sons are brought before him and Samuel looks at them and thinks that surely one of them is "the man".   This is what God say's though:

1 Samuel 16:7

But the Lord said to Samuel, "Do not look at his appearance or at the height of his stature, because I have rejected him; for God sees not as man sees, for man looks at the outward appearance, but the Lord looks at the heart."

Therefore, David is brought from the fields and presented to Samuel. God chooses David and his is anointed by Samuel to be the next King of Israel.

God now sets David on a path to interact with King Saul.

First David is brought to the palace to soothe the King with fine music when his mind is troubled.   This then sets up one of the most famous events in the bible.

David .vs Goliath.

We all know about David and Goliath, and the great victory that David had over the Philistine giant. Even today this story is used to describe any battle of small and weak .vs large and strong.

With one stone, David is able to encourage the entire army and they chase the Philistines army back to their own country.

While this is a famous story, fewer people have studied the relationship between David and Jonathan and know how Jonathan offered encouragement to David at a crucial time in his life.

You have to know that Jonathan is the son of King Saul and that would mean that he is next in line to be King. An appropriate title for Jonathan today would be Prince Jonathan. When his father died, he would be King of Israel. This is important to note, because it will help you to better understand how incredible it is that Jonathan becomes a key encourager in David's life.

Here is a brief set up of the events that lead to Jonathan encouraging David.

- David has slain Goliath
- Jonathan and David "become one in the spirit" and best friends
- Saul keeps David with him all the time now
- David and Jonathan become close friends
- The people praise David over King Saul for having killed more men
- King Saul becomes jealous and sets out to kill David
- King Saul pursues David to kill him

David is a young man and now fears for his life.

The KING wants him dead. Who wants to have the leader of a country as your enemy? I don't know about you, but I would be trembling with fear. Imagine making an enemy of the President of the United States and now his mission is to have you killed. He will use all of his resources at his disposal to end your life. Pretty scary stuff!

When you are in great fear of death, don't you think this would be a good time for encouragement?

Who would expect the encouragement to come from the Kings son???

He is next in line to be King and this is his father. However, Jonathan chooses loyalty to David. See how this starts to play out and note the final sentence in verse four.

1 Samuel 20:1-4

Then David fled from Naioth in Ramah, and came and said to Jonathan, "What have I done? What is my iniquity? And what is my sin before your father, that he is seeking my life?"
He said to him, "Far from it, you shall not die. Behold, my father does nothing either great or small without disclosing it to me. So why should my father hide this thing from me? It is not so!"

Yet David vowed again, saying, "Your father knows well that I have found favor in your sight, and he has said, 'Do not let Jonathan know this, or he will be grieved.' But truly as the Lord lives and as your soul lives, there is [hardly a step between me and death."

*Then Jonathan said to David, "**Whatever you say, I will do for you.**"*

The emphasis on the last sentence is mine as I want to point out what an incredible statement this is from Jonathan to David. Jonathan is willing to do whatever it takes to help his friend. I can only imagine how David's heart must have been encouraged by these words from his friend.

But Jonathan is not done encouraging David yet. David comes up with a simple plan for Jonathan to let him know if King Saul is really intent on killing him and if he should flee.

Without getting into all the details, Jonathan follows the instructions given to him by David and is able to warn David that the King is indeed intent on killing him.

This is where Jonathan gives David some parting words of encouragement.

1 Samuel 20:42

Jonathan said to David, "Go in safety, inasmuch as we have sworn to each other in the name of the Lord, saying, 'The Lord will be between me and you, and between my descendants and your descendants forever.'" Then he rose and departed, while Jonathan went into the city.

Jonathan does not yet know at this time that David is going to be King one day. He only knows that David is his friend. He is basically telling David that he and his family will have nothing to fear in the future when he is King. What powerful and incredible words! What a great friendship.

King Saul is now hunting David and pursues him across the country side. He finally finds out that David appears to be in the Desert of Ziph and is closing in, ready to strike him down once and for all.

In this final act of friendship, Jonathan seeks out David to offer these words of encouragement.

1 Samuel 23:15-18

Now David became aware that Saul had come out to seek his life while David was in the wilderness of Ziph at Horesh. And Jonathan, Saul's son, arose and went to David at Horesh, and encouraged him in God. Thus he said to him, "Do not be afraid, because the hand of Saul my father will not find you, and you will be king over Israel and I will be next to you; and Saul my father knows that also." So the two of them made a covenant before the Lord; and David stayed at Horesh while Jonathan went to his house.

Jonathan now knows that he will not be King of Israel. That mantle has passed to David. When you think about it, all Jonathan has to do is kill David and he would be the next King. However, Jonathan chooses friendship, loyalty and love over his own personal desires for success. He also must know that God has anointed David and to harm the "anointed one" would be a very serious sin.

I hope that you have a Jonathan in your life; someone who can offer you love and encouragement, even when it might not be in their best interest. Someone who has "got your back" and will always be do things that are in your best interest.

Or perhaps, you can be the Jonathan in someone's' life.

Look for those opportunities to offer encouragement to others especially when they are in danger and facing great adversity.   It is easy to be a friend in good times; it is much more difficult in times of trouble.

Blessing to you! Be encouraged!

Worksheet

Take time to answer the questions, pray and reflect on what you just read in this chapter and how you might apply the learning to your life.

Is there someone you know who is under great stress and needs encouragement?

What can you do to encourage them today?

Can you offer encouragement to someone today, even if it is not in your best interest?   Choose today to be a "Jonathan" in someone's life.

Solomon

A father's word to his son

David was king of Israel and a man after God's own heart. He had been leading the nation for years and wanted to honor God with a permanent temple for the Ark of the Covenant. He had a grand vision and desire to honor God with a magnificent building.

However, God had another plan for the temple and it would not involve King David. Instead it would involve his son Solomon. (Solomon was the second son born to David and Bathsheba)

We all know Solomon as the man of wisdom and riches. He wrote the book of Proverbs, Ecclesiastes and Song of Songs. However, when he is giving reign over Israel, he is a young man. None of the commentators I have read can agree on his age, but the general range is 12-20 years of age. To my way of thinking, that seems very young.

So, David wants to encourage his young son and set him up for success in life. He knows that Solomon is inexperienced and will need help building the temple.

1 Chronicles 22:5

David said, "My son Solomon is young and inexperienced, and the house that is to be built for the Lord shall be exceedingly magnificent, famous and glorious throughout all lands. Therefore now I will make preparation for it." So David made ample preparations before his death.

David is a good dad at this stage and is helping his son by making the preparations and helping to make his transition to leader more successful. A good father is always looking for ways to encourage and help his children grow and lead.

King David then calls his son Solomon and tells him that he will be the one building the temple. This must have put a bit of trepidation into Solomon to take on such a large task, but King David is going to encourage him and put his heart at ease.

1 Chronicles 22:11

*Now, my son, the Lord be with you that you may be successful, and build the house of the Lord your God just as He has spoken concerning you. Only the Lord give you discretion and understanding, and give you charge over Israel, so that you may keep the law of the Lord your God. Then you will prosper, if you are careful to observe the statutes and the ordinances which the Lord commanded Moses concerning Israel. **Be strong and courageous, do not fear nor be dismayed.***

Do those last words in his comments to his son look familiar?

Where have we seen them before?

These were the same words that Moses used to encourage Joshua as he was about take over leadership of the nation of Israel. My guess is that David was very familiar with the words of Moses to Joshua and chose the words very intentionally to encourage his young son.

Not only does David offer words of encouragement, he also sets about making the necessary preparations that will help his son be successful. He goes on to allocate money and resources to the endeavor. He also commands his leaders to come alongside his son to make him successful.

Finally as the time comes for Solomon to take on the project, King David has some last words of encouragement and advice for him.

1 Chronicles 28:9-10

"As for you, my son Solomon, know the God of your father, and serve Him with a whole heart and a willing mind; for the Lord searches all hearts, and understands every intent of the thoughts. If you seek Him, He will let you find Him; but if you forsake Him, He will reject you forever. Consider now, for the Lord has chosen you to build a house for the sanctuary; be courageous and act."

1 Chronicles 28:20-21

Then David said to his son Solomon, "Be strong and courageous, and act; do not fear nor be dismayed, for the Lord God, my God, is with you. He will not fail you nor forsake you until all the work for the service of the house of the Lord is finished. Now behold, there are the divisions of the priests and the Levites for all the service of the house of God, and every willing man of any skill will be with you in all the work for all kinds of service. The officials also and all the people will be entirely at your command."

What are the key words in these verses?

- Be Strong
- Be Courageous
- Act
- Do not Fear

He knew the effect these words would have on his son, and by repeating them several times throughout 1 Chronicles, he wanted them to sink in and encourage his son.

David certainly made many mistakes in his lifetime and I am sure that he had regrets, there is no doubt he loved his son Solomon and wanted him to be successful and more importantly be a great leader who would serve God.

As parents one our key jobs in life is to be an encourager to our children. We need to be their biggest cheerleader and advocate. We need to make sure we are setting them up for success and creating righteous pathways for them to follow.

This week think about how you can be a better encourager to your children (and your spouse). Be intentional about your encouragement and use all the technology at your disposal to encourage them. Text them, Tweet to them, write a note (pen and paper), call them, post a message on Facebook to them, and yes of course the face to face Interaction is the most important.

Here are King David's final words to his son just before he died:

1 Kings 2:1-4

As David's time to die drew near, he charged Solomon his son, saying, "I am going the way of all the earth. Be strong, therefore, and show yourself a man. Keep the charge of the Lord your God, to walk in His ways, to keep His statutes, His commandments, His ordinances, and His testimonies, according to what is written in the Law of Moses, that you may succeed in all that you do and wherever you turn, so that the Lord may carry out His promise which He spoke concerning me, saying, 'If your sons are careful of their way, to walk before Me in [truth with all their heart and with all their soul, you shall not lack a man on the throne of Israel.'

What sweet words to the ear of Solomon. David is offering the final advice for him to follow to be successful as leader and King.

Worksheet

Take time to answer the questions, pray and reflect on what you just read in this chapter and how you might apply the learning to your life.

Which of your children needs encouragement today?

How can you set them up for success?

What can you do to be a positive role model for your children when it comes to encouragement?

Mephibosheth

A father's legacy

Have you ever reaped the reward or blessing for something that you did not do?

Getting what you do not deserve is called Grace.   As Christians, we receive God's Grace through the redemptive power of His son Jesus Christ and the price he paid for our sins on the cross.

So who is Mephibosheth and how was he encouraged.

The story of Mephibosheth is told in 2 Samuel. He is a very minor character in the bible, but it is a powerful testament of love, devotion and faithfulness.

Mephibosheth was the son of Jonathan.   This is the same Jonathan that was the best friend of David.

When he was 5 years old, he we crippled in both legs as he and his nurse were fleeing.

Why were they fleeing?

Because his father (Jonathan), grandfather (King Saul) and uncles had all been killed and there was fear that all the family members would now be slaughtered.

Instead of death, he was crippled and then stuck in obscurity for many years and most likely glad to keep is head low and not be noticed by anybody.

And then the day of grace arrived for him.

David was now King, and had been doing battle and conquering the lands. His legend had grown even as the house of Saul had passed away.

David then remembers how well Jonathan had treated him when he was struggling and fleeing for his life when King Saul wanted to kill him. He then starts looking for a way to repay the kindness and loyalty that Jonathan has shown to him.

We pick up the story in 2 Samuel chapter 9:

2 Samuel 9:1-3

Then David said, "Is there yet anyone left of the house of Saul, that I may show him kindness for Jonathan's sake?" Now there was a servant of the house of Saul whose name was Ziba, and they called him to David; and the king said to him,

"Are you Ziba?" And he said, "I am your servant."

The king said, "Is there not yet anyone of the house of Saul to whom I may show the kindness of God?" And Ziba said to the king, "There is still a son of Jonathan who is crippled in both feet."

So David reached out to a servant of Saul because he was hoping that someone would have information that would help him find someone from Jonathan's family. You have to remember that Saul and Jonathan along with his brothers had all been killed in battle against the Philistines, and nobody was sure what happened to the family members.

Now David is ready to act:

2 Samuel 9:4-6

So the king said to him, "Where is he?" And Ziba said to the king, "Behold, he is in the house of Machir the son of Ammiel in Lo-debar." Then King David sent and brought him from the house of Machir the son of Ammiel, from Lo-debar. Mephibosheth, the son of Jonathan the son of Saul, came to David and fell on his face and prostrated himself. And David said, "Mephibosheth." And he said, "Here is your servant!"

What do your suppose was going through Mephibosheth's mind right now?

The Kings men had come for him and he knew that he was from the house and lineage of King Saul. In those days, it was customary for the new King to kill all of the descendants of the old King. My guess is that fear and dread we in his mind! He could not flee, as both of his legs were crippled.

He was at the mercy of the king.

Mephibosheth is now on his face and knows his life hangs in the balance. The next words from the King could be literally be the last words he ever hears.

What King David does next is remarkable

2 Samuel 9:7-13

David said to him, "Do not fear, for I will surely show kindness to you for the sake of your father Jonathan, and will restore to you all the land of your grandfather Saul; and you shall eat at my table regularly." Again he prostrated himself and said, "What is your servant, that you should regard a dead dog like me?"

Then the king called Saul's servant Ziba and said to him, "All that belonged to Saul and to all his house I have given to your master's grandson. You and your sons and your servants shall cultivate the land for him, and you shall bring in the produce so that your master's grandson may have food; nevertheless Mephibosheth your master's grandson shall eat at my table regularly." Now Ziba had fifteen sons and twenty servants.

Then Ziba said to the king, "According to all that my lord the king commands his servant so your servant will do." So Mephibosheth ate at David's table as one of the king's sons. Mephibosheth had a young son whose name was Mica. And all who lived in the house of Ziba were servants to Mephibosheth. So Mephibosheth lived in Jerusalem, for he ate at the king's table regularly. Now he was lame in both feet.

So King David gave him back his lands, gave him servants to work the land and invited him to be a regular guest at his table! Mephibosheth was expecting death, and instead he gets deliverance and is now a friend of the King.

Do you think Mephibosheth was encouraged by this act of grace and kindness?

Can you image how his heart must have leaped in his chest when King David basically made him just like a son!

Words are powerful things and can crush a person or build them up. The words from a King literally held the power of life and death.

In this instance it was abundant life. I am sure that Mephibosheth was grateful to his father and the legacy of love and kindness that he had shown King David. It was now being repaid to him and his family.

Jonathan had no way of knowing that the love, loyalty, encouragement and help he had given to David would be paid forward to his son. This is just another example of us not being able to see situations from end to end and because of this should encourage you to consider the impact of your actions on future generations.

What you say and do today, could very well impact a future that you may never live to see. Therefore, take every opportunity to offer encouragement and help.

As we close out this chapter take that time to ponder in your heart the Grace that God has given us and the simple story of King David and Mephibosheth.

Blessing to you! Be encouraged!

Worksheet

Take time to answer the questions, pray and reflect on what you just read in this chapter and how you might apply the learning to your life.

Is there someone in your life who has shown you kindness in the past?

Have you taken time to thank them lately?

If they are no longer around, is there someone in their life that you can encourage and show kindness to?

Is there someone you should reach out to with kindness and love for the sake of another?

Take time to pray and thank God for bringing people into your life who have encouraged you and shown kindness to you.

Mary
Reassurance for a young mom

Most scholars believe that Mary was a teenager when she became the mother of Jesus. I don't know about you, but when I was a teenager I was not even prepared to take care of myself, much less a family.

As a father with two teenage daughters, I cannot begin to imagine what might have been going through her heart and mind as she went through this phase of her life. I am sure her heart and mind were filled with all manner of thoughts, fears and doubts.

I do know that it would have been important for her to be encouraged during this critical time in her life.

After the angel Gabriel spoke to Mary and told her that she would be the mother of Jesus, she immediately went to see her cousin Elizabeth.

Why did she go?

- Gabriel had told her that Elizabeth was expecting a child (even in her old age)
- Mary would have wanted to have someone to talk to and confide in
- Mary knew that Elizabeth would most likely be sympathetic
- Mary would need some help in the 1st trimester as this can sometimes be very challenging.

So Mary goes to Elizabeth not knowing what to expect. Will she be welcomed? Will she be criticized, ostracized?

What she receives is encouragement and reassurance when she sees her cousin Elizabeth.

Luke 1:39-45

Now at this time Mary arose and went in a hurry to the hill country, to a city of Judah, and entered the house of Zacharias and greeted Elizabeth. When Elizabeth heard Mary's greeting, the baby leaped in her womb; and Elizabeth was filled with the Holy Spirit. And she cried out with a loud voice and said, "Blessed are you among women, and blessed is the fruit of your womb! And how has it happened to me, that the mother of my Lord would come to me? For behold, when the sound of your greeting reached my ears, the baby leaped in my womb for joy. And blessed is she who believed that there would be a fulfillment of what had been spoken to her by the Lord."

So now Mary knows that what she heard from Gabriel is true and God has given her reassurance and encouragement through the words of her cousin Elizabeth.

She stays with Elizabeth for three months and then returns home and time passes by.

A census is now required throughout the land and she and Joseph went to Bethlehem (because that was his home town) to be counted.

While there she gave birth to Jesus and a group of shepherds came to see the baby and proclaim to all what had happened that night.

Luke 2:17-19

When they (the shepherds) *had seen this* (Mary and the Baby*), they made known the statement which had been told them about this Child. And all who heard it wondered at the things which were told them by the shepherds. But Mary treasured all these things, pondering them in her heart.*

Now not only had Mary heard from her cousin Elizabeth, but now some local shepherds had also spoken about Jesus and how special he was, that He was the Christ. It then says that Mary pondered this in her heart. I like to think that this is just another example of God reassuring a young mother and encouraging her.

A lot has been happening and eight days quickly pass since the shepherds had come to see her and Jesus in the manger. It is time to take the baby to temple to be circumcised. This is a pretty normal event in a Jewish baby's life.

However, God is going to continue to encourage and reassure Mary by having a righteous man named Simeon speak into her life.

Simeon had been reassured by the Holy Spirit that he would not die before he saw the Lord Christ. Simeon was at the temple the day when Jesus was brought to be circumcised. See what happens next:

Luke 2:27-33

And he (Simeon) came in the Spirit into the temple; and when the parents brought in the child Jesus, to carry out for Him the custom of the Law, then he took Him into his arms, and blessed God, and said,

"Now Lord, You are releasing Your bond-servant to depart in peace, According to Your word; For my eyes have seen Your salvation, Which You have prepared in the presence of all peoples, A Light of revelation to the Gentiles, And the glory of Your people Israel."

And His father and mother were amazed at the things which were being said about Him.

So, once again God uses an individual to speak into Mary's life and encourage here in regard to her baby boy.

As some more time passes, Mary is about to be encouraged and reassured by a group of Magi (wise men).

Most scholars believe that Jesus would have been 1-2 years old by the time the Magi sought him out to bring him gifts and worship him.

Matthew 2:7-11

Then Herod secretly called the magi and determined from them the exact time the star appeared. And he sent them to Bethlehem and said, "Go and search carefully for the Child; and when you have found Him, report to me, so that I too may come and worship Him." After hearing the king, they went their way; and the star, which they had seen in the east, went on before them until it came and stood over the place where the Child was. When they saw the star, they rejoiced exceedingly with great joy. After coming into the house they saw the Child with Mary His mother; and they fell to the ground and worshiped Him. Then, opening their treasures, they presented to Him gifts of gold, frankincense, and myrrh.

Mary would have been going through all the usual paces of a young mother and wife during this time; making a home, taking care of a young child and being a young bride.

In other words, she would a have been very busy just taking care of the day to day duties and not really thinking about the future. What an incredible opportunity for God to encourage and reassure her of who her son was and how special he would be.

Think about all the different people God used to encourage and reassure a young mother:

- Elizabeth her cousin - before he is born
- Shepard boys - at his birth
- Simeon - at the temple
- Magi - as a toddler

Consider who God uses to offer Mary encouragement:

✓ A close family member
✓ Poor strangers (very lowly in stature)
✓ A Godly/Righteous man
✓ Rich Wise men

In other words, she has been encouraged by the major facets of society at that time. God clearly wanted her to receive the message of encouragement for a very eclectic group of individuals, so that she would have to know it was from God.

I believe that God knew that Mary would need each of these instances to encourage her and reassure her of the words she first heard from Gabriel at the very beginning.

God is good all the time!

Blessing to you! Be encouraged!

Worksheet

Take time to answer the questions, pray and reflect on what you just read in this chapter and how you might apply the learning to your life.

Is there someone you know who is in a difficult circumstance that you can encourage - even when others have abandoned them?

Are you in a difficult circumstance and need encouragement?   Is there someone in your life you can turn to and seek encouragement?

Is there an opportunity of you to be an "Elizabeth" to someone else?

Take time now to pray for all those who face difficult times.

•

Saul

Many helpers along the way

This is not King Saul of the Old Testament; this is Saul of the New Testament. This is Saul, who would one day become the Apostle Paul the prolific writer of the New Testament.

Saul was originally a bitter enemy of the early church and set out to destroy the church and anybody associated with it. He was there when Stephen became the first martyr and was stoned to death.

However, God had a plan to greatly use Saul to spread the good news of the Gospel of Jesus Christ.

On the road to Damascus (where Saul is headed to persecute Christians), he is blinded by the Lord and had to be led by hand into the city. For three days he was in this condition (I think it is very interesting that God choose three days for Saul to suffer - the same amount of time that Jesus spent from his death until his resurrection).

Can you image being blind for three days? Saul must have had plenty of time to pray, think, and contemplate his past life.

God is about to start encouraging Saul through two men who will come alongside him (even though many feared him because of his reputation).

Suddenly, God sends a disciple named Ananias to lay hands on Saul to heal him of his blindness. What joy and relief Saul must have felt. It was also a confirmation of the vision God had given him that a man named Ananias was going to help him.

Do you think Saul was encouraged? Do you think others around him were encouraged as well? Saul once was blind, but now he "sees" for the first time in his life.

Acts 9:26-28

So Ananias departed and entered the house, and after laying his hands on him said, "Brother Saul, the Lord Jesus, who appeared to you on the road by which you were coming, has sent me so that you may regain your sight and be filled with the Holy Spirit."

And immediately there fell from his eyes something like scales, and he regained his sight, and he got up and was baptized; and he took food and was strengthened.

Saul stays in Damascus for a short time, until his life is threatened and then he know he must flee.

Saul heads to Jerusalem and he tries to join the disciples and is hit with the reality of his past reputation.

They all feared him. Saul must have been crushed and very disappointed. He knew that he was a changed man, but he now had to deal with the consequences of his past deeds.

Lucky for Saul, there was a man there who was about to give him his greatest encouragement yet!

Acts 9:26-28

When he came to Jerusalem, he was trying to associate with the disciples; but they were all afraid of him, not believing that he was a disciple. But Barnabas took hold of him and brought him to the apostles and described to them how he had seen the Lord on the road, and that He had talked to him, and how at Damascus he had spoken out boldly in the name of Jesus. And he was with them, moving about freely in Jerusalem, speaking out boldly in the name of the Lord.

Notice how it says that Barnabas "took hold of him" and brought him to the apostles. Why did Barnabas have to take hold of him?

My guess is that Saul was dejected and did not want to go. He had tried it on his own and the people feared him. Why would anyone sign up for more rejection??

Barnabas went out a limb and spoke up for Saul. Not only did he "vouch" for him, but he praised him for his bold stance in Damascus for the cause of Christ.

Barnabas truly earned his nickname "son of encouragement" with these words to the apostles. Saul is sitting there in front of the apostle of Christ and here he is being spoken about positively.

Proverbs 27:2

Let another praise you, and not your own mouth; A stranger, and not your own lips

Saul's heart must have soared that day! God used Barnabas to speak encouragement into his life at a crucial time of his conversion.

Saul is sent home to Tarsus because of the threats to his life. Later Barnabas joins him for a year and they move to Antioch where the believers are first called Christians.

After that, Saul and Barnabas go on to make the first missionary journey together. What a great companion Barnabas must have been for Paul in those early years. God knew that Saul would need lots of encouragement as they faced many trials and obstacles as they preached and taught the Good News of Jesus Christ.

Saul eventually changes his name to Paul and takes a young disciple under his wing by the name of Timothy. Paul goes on to pen two letters of encouragement to Timothy (1st and 2nd Timothy in our bible). I would like to think that Paul's ability to encourage was a direct result of having been influenced by Barnabas. In other words he was "paying it forward".

Has someone encouraged you in your life? Have you thanked them lately? Is there someone you can encourage and "pay forward" the encouragement that was brought into your life?

Take the time now to thank God for those encouragers he has brought into your life.

Blessing to you! Be encouraged!

<u>Worksheet</u>

Take time to answer the questions, pray and reflect on what you just read in this chapter and how you might apply the learning to your life.

Is there a new believer that you can encourage today?

Are you a new believer that needs encouragement?

Take time now to pray for others who you know need encouragement.

Timothy

A mentor speaks

Have you ever had a mentor in your life?

Have you been a mentor to someone?

We all need positive mentors in our life to help guide and direct us on the right path.   A good mentor always has our best interest in mind and only wants to see us be successful and do well.   A good mentor is also not afraid to correct us and offer discipline when necessary.

Timothy was a young Christian who was positively influenced by both his mother and grandmother.   He also had a mentor in the apostle Paul.   Paul felt so close to Timothy that he referred to him as "son".

In the books of 1st and 2nd Timothy Paul offers much encouragement to Timothy.   As you read these words of encouragement, think of the many "Timothy's" in your life and how you can speak words of encouragement to them.

Paul tells Timothy to - Fight the good fight!

1 Timothy 1:18-19

This command I entrust to you, Timothy, my son, in accordance with the prophecies previously made concerning you, that by them you fight the good fight, keeping faith and a good conscience, which some have rejected and suffered shipwreck in regard to their faith.

Paul tells Timothy - Do not worry about what others think!

1 Timothy 4:12

Let no one look down on your youthfulness, but rather in speech, conduct, love, faith and purity, show yourself an example of those who believe.

Paul tells him again - Fight the good fight!

1 Timothy 6:12

Fight the good fight of faith; take hold of the eternal life to which you were called, and you made the good confession in the presence of many witnesses.

Paul encourages him - You have incredible faith!

2 Timothy 1:5

For I am mindful of the sincere faith within you, which first dwelt in your grandmother Lois and your mother Eunice, and I am sure that it is in you as well.

Paul tells Timothy - Be Strong!

2 Timothy 2:1-7

You therefore, my son, be strong in the grace that is in Christ Jesus. The things which you have heard from me in the presence of many witnesses, entrust these to faithful men who will be able to teach others also. Suffer hardship with me, as a good soldier of Christ Jesus. No soldier in active service entangles himself in the affairs of everyday life, so that he may please the one who enlisted him as a soldier. Also if anyone competes as an athlete, he does not win the prize unless he competes according to the rules. The hard-working farmer ought to be the first to receive his share of the crops. Consider what I say, for the Lord will give you understanding in everything.

Paul uses very powerful words to speak encouragement into Timothy's life. He does not pull any punches, but is loving and kind as he offers his advice and counsel.

The books for 1st and 2nd Timothy offer many more lesson and teaching beyond these few words for encouragement. Paul was very concerned with Timothy's spiritual growth and maturity and wants him to finish well.

I should note that all of these words are in the forms of letters that Paul had written to Timothy. He was not there in person, so he did the next best thing he could do at this time and that was to write a letter.

You should use every form of communication at your disposal when you are trying to encourage someone. Just because you are not with them in person, does not be you cannot encourage them.

My oldest daughter took the opportunity to write me a letter that she wanted me to open in the future. It was specifically labeled "Open when you really miss me". She is away at college, so I seldom see her these days. Then one day, I was very discouraged and was missing my daughter and I remembered her letter. I opened the letter and it was filled with love and encouragement. I wept tears of joy and happiness. My daughter was so thoughtful and of course the timing was perfect.

My hope and prayer is that you will fight the good fight and finish well. Look for the opportunity to be a mentor and pray that God would send a mentor into your life. We all need someone in our life to encourage, challenge and help us through this life.

Blessing to you! Be encouraged!

Worksheet

Take time to answer the questions, pray and reflect on what you just read in this chapter and how you might apply the learning to your life.

Are you a mentor to someone?   How you encourage your mentee today?

If you do not have a mentee, work with your church to see if they have a formal program that you can engage in.

Do you have a mentor in your life?   If not, pray now that God would send a mentor to help you through all aspects of your life.

Joseph
A well deserved name

Did you ever have a nickname?

What does it take to get a nickname?

Usually it has something to do with an accomplishment, your physical appearance or attribute.

I had a bunch of different nicknames growing up, but most of them I did not appreciate.

Here are a few famous nicknames in recent history:

Nickname	Real Name
The Lone Eagle	Charles Lindbergh
The Wizard of Menlo Park	Thomas Edison
The Sultan of Swat	George Herman Ruth
The Intimidator	Dale Earnhardt Sr.
The Moses of Her People	Harriet Tubman
Buffalo Bill	William Cody
Angel of the Battlefield	Clara Barton
The Great Emancipator	Abraham Lincoln
Ol' Blue Eyes	Frank Sinatra
Hammering Hank	Hank Aaron
Pistol Pete	Pete Marovich
The King of Rock n Roll	Elvis
The Red Baron	Manfred von Richthofen
Stonewall Jackson	Thomas Jonathan Jackson

Each of these individuals earned their nickname by their unique achievements. Some flew airplanes, some played sports, some were soldiers and others were entertainers.

One thing that is true of all of them is that throughout history their nicknames will follow them and some people may not even know their real name.   For better or worse they nickname is theirs forever!

In the bible a number of people had their name changed (many of them because they were in captivity).

Daniel	renamed	Belshazzar
Hananiah	renamed	Shadrach
Mishael	renamed	Meshach
Azariah	renamed	Abednego
Joseph	renamed	Zaphenath-Paneah

Others in the New Testament had their nicknames as well:

Simon (which means "reed like "or "grass like") became Peter - or Rock - not a common name in that age and it would be the equivalent of calling someone "concrete" today.   It spoke to his changing character as he grew and matured as a believer and apostle of Christ.

James and John became the Boanerges or "Sons of Thunder" - James was the first martyr and John became the apostle of Love.

However, my favorite bible character who had a different name was Joseph of the New Testament.   I am not talking about Jesus's earthly father Joseph.   I am referring to Barnabas.   Most people only know him by the name Barnabas, but his real name was Joseph.

What does Barnabas mean?

The name Barnabas is a Hebrew baby name. In Hebrew the meaning of the name Barnabas is: Son of consolation or son of exhortation, son of comfort.

However in the book of acts this is how his name is described:

Acts 4:36

Now Joseph, a Levite of Cyprian birth, who was also called Barnabas by the apostles (which translated means Son of Encouragement),

The word for encouragement that is used in the Greek is παρακλησις (paraklesis), meaning the act of exhorting, encouraging or comforting.

This is a very interesting word to use, because it is the same root word used to describe the Holy Spirit. In other words, this is an awesome nickname to have.

It is quite an honor to be known throughout all of history as the Son of Encouragement. That is quite a testimony to his life and service. So how did he get the name?

There are a couple of specific things that he did that would point to his efforts to encourage others.

- He sold a field to help the early Christian believers in Jerusalem
- He was the one who introduced Paul to the Apostles in Jerusalem when they were too afraid of Paul and did not believe he had been converted
- It was Barnabas who went to Tarsus to get Paul to come help with the work in Antioch
- He accompanied Paul on the first missionary journey
- He Encouraged Mark to join the missionary journey, and stood by him when Paul did not want Mark with them on a second mission trip (because Mark had failed to complete the first trip)

It is easy to see why he would earn his nickname. He is using his time, talents and treasures to encourage others. He is loyal and brave and not afraid to stand up and defend others. He is a great example for all of us to follow.

What will your legacy be with your friends, family, neighbors and co-workers? Will they remember you as someone who encouraged others? What can you do today to encourage others? Take the time to be intentional about your encouragement.

Blessing to you! Be encouraged!

Worksheet

Take time to answer the questions, pray and reflect on what you just read in this chapter and how you might apply the learning to your life.

Are you a Barnabas? How can you be an even better Barnabas?

Do you have a Barnabas in your life? If yes, praise God and thank Him for sending you a Barnabas. If not, pray that God would send a Barnabas into your life.

Proactively seek out others today that you can become a Barnabas to.

Here are a few people that you can think about being a Barnabas to:

- Pastor/Preacher
- Teacher
- Neighbor
- Co-worker

Jesus

Words of encouragement

If you had a good friend call you and tell you that they were overwhelmed and in great sorrow, and needed you by their side, would you go to them? Would you think that they would be in need of encouragement and comfort? I bet you would and I bet you would go to their side.

Amazingly, this is where we find Jesus. He has just finished his last supper with the disciples, Judas has left to betray him and He is headed to the Garden of Gethsemane to pray. Jesus knows he only has a few precious hours to live and he knows the agony that is coming his way. He desired to have three friends close by in this final phase of his ministry. He took Peter, John and James with him deeper into the garden (it was these three who had seen his transfiguration). He clearly wanted them close by, both for encouragement and comfort as well as to continue teaching them even in these last hours.

Here we pick up the story from Matthew as Jesus head into the garden to pray:

Matthew 26:38

Then He said to them, "My soul is deeply grieved, to the point of death; remain here and keep watch with Me."

Here are some other translations for the word "grieved" used in Matthew:

Overwhelmed
Crushed
Sorrowful
Anguish

No matter the translation, it is clear that our Lord was hurting. Having his disciples close by during this time would be both an encouragement and a comfort. Jesus was setting yet another good example for us; that in our time of need we do not need to be alone, but should seek to surround ourselves with close friends who will "keep watch".

In the book of Luke we find something that is not in Matthew, Mark or John. We see that as Jesus continues to pray and is giving himself into His fathers will, he needs to be strengthened for the final hours. God is such a good father that he wants to help Jesus endure the unendurable and sends an angel to strengthen him in those last hours.

It is this final bit of encouragement that will help propel our Lord forward into death and then glorious resurrection. As the Son of God, he would not have needed this, but as a man, clothed in the same flesh as the rest of us, it was a necessary last bit of preparation.

Luke 22:41-43

And He withdrew from them about a stone's throw, and He knelt down and began to pray, saying, "Father, if You are willing, remove this cup from Me; yet not My will, but Yours be done." Now an angel from heaven appeared to Him, strengthening Him.

To God be the glory, great things he has done! If even our Lord needed encouragement, how much more do we need encouragement!

Jesus's Words of Encouragement

Of course Jesus is our advocate, sitting at the right hand of the Father making intercession for us. While he was here on earth, he offered some very specific words of encouragement:

.
- I will give you rest
- Don't worry about tomorrow
- I have overcome this world
- No one can snatch you out of my hand
- I have prepared a place for you
- I am with your always, even to the end of the age (or world)

What Jesus is offering us in these words of encouragement are aspects of his character that will impact the key areas of our life. We let our guard down when we are tired or worried and start to become discouraged. Jesus gives us something to look forward to in the future, while assuring us he will help us in the here and now.

Matthew 11:28-30

"Come to Me, all who are weary and heavy-laden, and I will give you rest. Take My yoke upon you and learn from Me, for I am gentle and humble in heart, and you will find rest for your souls. For My yoke is easy and My burden is light."

I know that when I am tired I make bad decisions, have poor judgment and generally just not a pleasant person to be around. Rest is so critical in our life. We need a minimum of 7 hours of sleep each day for our body to function properly. Even God rested on the 7th day and set the example for us to take time out to slow down.

Here, Christ is telling us to lay our burdens on him (the yoke is symbolic of our trials and troubles) and we can find rest!

John 16:33

These things I have spoken to you, so that in Me you may have peace. In the world you have tribulation, but take courage; I have overcome the world."

We fear the unknown and enemies seen and not seen. Chris is simply telling us "I got your back". It is easy to forget (when we have the weight of the world on our shoulders) that our God is THE God and he has overcome the world and we are more the conquers with Him.

Matthew 6:31-34

Do not worry then, saying, 'What will we eat?' or 'What will we drink?' or 'What will we wear for clothing?' For the Gentiles eagerly seek all these things; for your heavenly Father knows that you need all these things. But seek first His kingdom and His righteousness, and all these things will be added to you. "So do not worry about tomorrow; for tomorrow will care for itself. Each day has enough trouble of its own.

How many of us worry about tomorrow, or the next week or year. Christ is reassuring us that if we put our complete trust and faith in him that he will take care of us.

John 10:27-28

My sheep hear My voice, and I know them, and they follow Me; and I give eternal life to them, and they will never perish; and no one will snatch them out of My hand.

Christ is our protector! We will have many enemies who will try to steal, kill and destroy, but Christ is offering us the protection for here and now and also for eternity.   This is incredibly comforting on so many levels.   I think about my children and know that I would do anything to protect them.   They know this as well, and because of that reassurance, the can sleep well and not worry about harm coming their way.   We all need, want and desire a protector in our life and Christ is there to answer the call.

John 14:1-6

"Do not let your heart be troubled; believe in God, believe also in Me. In My Father's house are many dwelling places; if it were not so, I would have told you; for I go to prepare a place for you. If I go and prepare a place for you, I will come again and receive you to Myself, that where I am, there you may be also. And you know the way where I am going." Thomas *said to Him, "Lord, we do not know where You are going, how do we know the way? "Jesus *said to him, "I am the way, and the truth, and the life; no one comes to the Father but through Me.

We all desire to know that our future is secure.   In these few passages, Christ is letting us know that our future is secure in and through Him. Christ knew that we would wonder about life after death and he is offering the hope of what is to come.   When we offer hope, we offer encouragement for the future and the desire to continue down the righteous path of life.

Matthew 28:16-20

But the eleven disciples proceeded to Galilee, to the mountain which Jesus had designated. When they saw Him, they worshiped Him; but some were doubtful. And Jesus came up and spoke to them, saying, "All authority has been given to Me in heaven and on earth. Go therefore and make disciples of all the nations, baptizing them in the name of the Father and the Son and the Holy Spirit, teaching them to observe all that I commanded you; and lo, I am with you always, even to the end of the age."

"even to the end of the age"
"Even unto the end of the world"
"Until the end of time"

Whether the translation is age, world or time, it is clear that Jesus was trying to encourage us with the fact the he will be with us FOREVER!

Hebrews 13:8

Jesus Christ is the same yesterday and today and forever.

As you read these words, I hope and pray that you are encouraged and know that Jesus loves you so very much!

Blessing to you! Be encouraged!

Worksheet

Take time to answer the questions, pray and reflect on what you just read in this chapter and how you might apply the learning to your life.

Do you need to be encouraged today?

What areas of your life do you need encouragement in?

- Relational - Family and Friends
- Financial - personal and or business
- Physical - your health or someone close to you
- Mental - your thought life
- Spiritual - prayer life, walking with God, study, worship
- Occupational - your job or business

List specifically the areas where you need encouragement and then pray over that list - specifically asking for encouragement.

Who can you encourage today?

I have found that when I am proactively seeking to encourage others, that more encouragement comes my way. Take the time today to be proactive in your encouragement.

Here are some Proactive ways to encourage:

- Hand written note
- Text
- Phone call
- Personal visit
- A timely gift
- Financial assistance
- Using social media

Different Types of Encouragement

In this book, I have outlined and discussed a number of different ways that people were encouraged.   In this final section, I will bring it all together and encourage you to incorporate these different methods into your life as you strive to encourage others. Obviously most of these characters were encouraged by words so I will not include that method in the list below:

Encouragement just by being available and mere presence

Adam and Eve
Moses and Aaron
Job and his friends
Mary and Elizabeth
Naomi and Ruth
Barnabas and Saul

Encouragement through a letter (use whatever you have)

Paul to Timothy

Encouragement by being physically helped

Moses with Aaron and Hur
Beggar with Peter and John
Ananias to Saul

Encouragement through selflessness

David and Jonathan
Naomi and Ruth
Barnabas and Saul

Encouragement with tangible gifts and help

Boaz and Ruth
Magi and Mary
Barnabas and early church members
David to Solomon

Encouragement as an act of grace and mercy

Joseph with his brothers
David with Mephibosheth

Encouragement for the future

Joseph with his brothers
David with Mephibosheth
Jesus to believers

Encouragement from Mentor to Mentee (son or daughter also)

Moses to Joshua
Paul to Timothy
Naomi to Ruth
David to Solomon
Barnabas to Saul

Obviously these two methods are not available for us to use

Encouragement directly from God

Moses
Mary
Gideon
Joshua

Encouragement through miracles

Moses
Gideon

Encouraging Quotes

There is only one way to avoid criticism: do nothing, say nothing, and be nothing. –**Aristotle**

Believe you can and you're halfway there. –**Theodore Roosevelt**

Winning isn't everything, but wanting to win is. –**Vince Lombardi**

Never consider the possibility of failure; as long as you persist, you will be successful. - **Brian Tracy**

Fall seven times, stand up eight. ~**Japanese Proverb**

Few things can help an individual more than to place responsibility on him, and to let him know that you trust him. –**Booker T. Washington**

One has to remember that every failure can be a stepping stone to something better. **Col. Harland Sanders**

A diamond is merely a lump of coal that did well under pressure. **Unknown**

Encouraging Quotes

It is not the mountain we conquer but ourselves.
Edmund Hillary

The best time to plant a tree was 20 years ago. The second best time is now. **Chinese Proverb**

Never give up on what you really want to do. The person with big dreams is more powerful than one with all the facts. - **Unknown**

If the wind will not serve, take to the oars. - **Latin Proverb**

*An unexamined life is not worth living. –***Socrates**

When you encourage others, you in the process are encouraged because you're making a commitment and difference in that person's life. Encouragement really does make a difference. **Zig Ziglar**

*You can't fall if you don't climb. But there's no joy in living your whole life on the ground. –***Unknown**

''Age is no barrier. It's a limitation you put on your mind.'' -
Jackie Joyner-Kersee

Do what you can, where you are, with what you have. –
Teddy Roosevelt

Encouraging Quotes

A word of encouragement from a teacher to a child can change a life. A word of encouragement from a spouse can save a marriage. A word of encouragement from a leader can inspire a person to reach her potential. **John C. Maxwell**

*Nothing is impossible, the word itself says, I'm possible! –***Audrey Hepburn**

Nine tenths of education is encouragement.
Anatole France

If you're going through hell, keep going. **-Winston Churchill**

*Either write something worth reading or do something worth writing. –***Benjamin Franklin**

I ask not for a lighter burden, but for broader shoulders.
-Jewish Proverb

*Everything will be OK in the end, if it's not OK, it's not the end.'' -***Unknown**

If you are a leader, you should never forget that everyone needs encouragement. And everyone who receives it - young or old, successful or less-than-successful, unknown or famous - is changed by it. **John C. Maxwell**

Encouraging Quotes

When you come to the end of your rope, tie a knot and hang on. - **Franklin D. Roosevelt**

*Twenty years from now you will be more disappointed by the things that you didn't do than by the ones you did do, so throw off the bowlines, sail away from safe harbor, catch the trade winds in your sails. Explore, Dream, Discover. – **Mark Twain***

*If you can dream it, you can achieve it. – **Zig Ziglar***

If you want to lift yourself up, lift up someone else. *–**Booker T. Washington***

*Don't be discouraged. It's often the last key in the bunch that opens the lock. - **Unknown***

*Two roads diverged in a wood, and I – I took the one less traveled by, And that has made all the difference. –**Robert Frost***

A person who never made a mistake never tried anything new. – **Albert Einstein**

*When one door closes another door opens; but we so often look so long and so regretfully upon the closed door, that we do not see the ones which open for us. - **Alexander Graham Bell***

Encouraging Quotes

Instruction does much, but encouragement everything.
— Johann Wolfgang von Goethe

Instead of giving myself reasons why I can't, I give myself reasons why I can. - **Author Unknown**

Education costs money. But then so does ignorance. –**Sir Claus Moser**

You miss 100% of the shots you don't take. –**Wayne Gretzky**

Whether you think you can or you think you can't, you're right. –
Henry Ford

A bend in the road is not the end of the road... unless you fail to make the turn. - **Unknown**

Life is 10% what happens to me and 90% of how I react to it. –
Charles Swindoll

Remember no one can make you feel inferior without your consent. –
Eleanor Roosevelt

Encouraging Quotes

I don't regret the things I've done, I regret the things I didn't do when I had the chance. – **Unknown**

You can never cross the ocean until you have the courage to lose sight of the shore. –**Christopher Columbus**

When it is dark enough, you can see the stars.
Ralph Waldo Emerson

In order to succeed, your desire for success should be greater than your fear of failure. – **Bill Cosby**

The difficulties of life are intended to make us better, not bitter.
Unknown

The pessimist sees difficulty in every opportunity. The optimist sees opportunity in every difficulty - **Winston Churchill**

I'd rather be a failure at something I love than a success at something I hate. - **George Burns**

I didn't fail the test. I just found 100 ways to do it wrong. –
Benjamin Franklin

Encouraging Quotes

People often say that motivation doesn't last. Well, neither does bathing. That's why we recommend it daily. **–Zig Ziglar**

It does not matter how slowly you go as long as you do not stop. – **Confucius**

You may not realize it when it happens, but a kick in the teeth may be the best thing in the world for you. **Walt Disney**

It's not the years in your life that count. It's the life in your years. – **Abraham Lincoln**

When you feel like giving up, remember why you held on for so long in the first place. - **Unknown**

Life is short, live it. Love is rare, grab it. Anger is bad, dump it. Fear is awful, face it. Memories are sweet, cherish it. – **Unknown**

Character cannot be developed in ease and quiet. Only through experience of trial and suffering can the soul be strengthened, ambition inspired, and success achieved.- **Helen Keller**

Rock bottom is good solid ground, and a dead end street is just a place to turn around. **-Buddy Buie and J.R. Cobb**

Encouraging Quotes

Do you give as much energy to your dreams as you do to your fears?
Unknown

Life is short, fragile and does not wait for anyone. There will NEVER be a perfect time to pursue your dreams & goals.
Unknown

Don't say you don't have enough time. You have exactly the same number of hours per day that were given to Helen Keller, Bill Gates, Michelangelo, Mother Teresa, Leonardo da Vinci, Thomas Jefferson, and Albert Einstein. **Unknown**

Even the greatest was once a beginner. Don't be afraid to take that first step. **Unknown**

The first to apologize is the bravest. The first to forgive is the strongest. The first to forget is the happiest.
Unknown

Never get tired of doing little things for your spouse. Sometimes those little things occupy the biggest part of their heart. **Unknown**

There is nothing more admirable than two people who see eye-to-eye keeping house as man and wife, confounding their enemies, and delighting their friends. **Homer**

Encouraging Quotes

When I am with you, the only place I want to be is closer.
Unknown

Marriage succeeds only as lifetime commitment with no escape clauses. **Dr. James Dobson**

A wise physician once said, 'The best medicine for humans is love.' Someone asked, 'What if it doesn't work?' He smiled and answered, 'Increase the dose'. **Unknown**

I want a marriage more beautiful than my wedding.
Unknown

Marriage is like a fine wine, if tended properly, it just gets better with age. **Unknown**

*Don't marry the person you think you can live with; marry only the individual you think you can't live without.-***James C. Dobson**

Love is just a word until someone comes along and gives it meaning.
Unknown

Lean on each other's strengths. Forgive each other's weaknesses.
Unknown

Encouraging Scripture

Matthew 11:28-30
"Come to Me, all who are weary and heavy-laden, and I will give you rest. Take My yoke upon you and learn from Me, for I am gentle and humble in heart, and you will find rest for your souls. For My yoke is easy and My burden is light."

Romans 8:28
And we know that God causes all things to work together for good to those who love God, to those who are called according to His purpose.

Ephesians 5:25
Husbands, love your wives, just as Christ also loved the church and gave Himself up for her,

1 Peter 5:7
Casting all your anxiety on Him, because He cares for you.

1 Thessalonians 5:9-11
For God has not destined us for wrath, but for obtaining salvation through our Lord Jesus Christ, who died for us, so that whether we are awake or asleep, we will live together with Him. Therefore encourage one another and build up one another, just as you also are doing.

Encouraging Scripture

2 Corinthians 4:16-18

Therefore we do not lose heart, but though our outer man is decaying, yet our inner man is being renewed day by day. For momentary, light affliction is producing for us an eternal weight of glory far beyond all comparison, while we look not at the things which are seen, but at the things which are not seen; for the things which are seen are temporal, but the things which are not seen are eternal.

2 Thessalonians 2:16-17

Now may our Lord Jesus Christ Himself and God our Father, who has loved us and given us eternal comfort and good hope by grace, comfort and strengthen your hearts in every good work and word.

2 Thessalonians 3:16

Now may the Lord of peace Himself continually grant you peace in every] circumstance. The Lord be with you all!

2 Timothy 1:7

For God has not given us a spirit of timidity, but of power and love and discipline.

Colossians 3:15

Let the peace of Christ rule in your hearts, to which indeed you were called in one body; and be thankful.

Encouraging Scripture

Deuteronomy 31:6
Be strong and courageous, do not be afraid or tremble at them, for the Lord your God is the one who goes with you. He will not fail you or forsake you."

Ephesians 4:2-3
with all humility and gentleness, with patience, showing tolerance for one another in love, being diligent to preserve the unity of the Spirit in the bond of peace.

Galatians 6:9
Let us not lose heart in doing good, for in due time we will reap if we do not grow weary.

Hebrews 10:25
not forsaking our own assembling together, as is the habit of some, but encouraging one another; and all the more as you see the day drawing near.

Hebrews 13:8
Jesus Christ is the same yesterday and today and forever.

Hebrews 6:18
 so that by two unchangeable things in which it is impossible for God to lie, we who have taken refuge would have strong encouragement to take hold of the hope set before us.

Encouraging Scripture

Isaiah 40:31
Yet those who wait for the Lord
Will gain new strength;
They will mount up with wings like eagles,
They will run and not get tired,
They will walk and not become weary.

Isaiah 41:10
'Do not fear, for I am with you;
Do not anxiously look about you, for I am your God.
I will strengthen you, surely I will help you,
Surely I will uphold you with My righteous right hand.'

Isaiah 41:13
"For I am the Lord your God, who upholds your right hand,
Who says to you, 'Do not fear, I will help you.'

James 1:2-4
Consider it all joy, my brethren, when you encounter various
trials, knowing that the testing of your faith produces
endurance. And let endurance have its perfect result, so that
you may be perfect and complete, lacking in nothing.

John 14:27
Peace I leave with you; My peace I give to you; not as the
world gives do I give to you. Do not let your heart be
troubled, nor let it be fearful.

Encouraging Scripture

Jeremiah 29:11-14
For I know the plans that I have for you,' declares the Lord, 'plans for welfare and not for calamity to give you a future and a hope. Then you will call upon Me and come and pray to Me, and I will listen to you. You will seek Me and find Me when you search for Me with all your heart. I will be found by you,' declares the Lord, 'and I will restore your fortunes and will gather you from all the nations and from all the places where I have driven you,' declares the Lord, 'and I will bring you back to the place from where I sent you into exile.'

John 14:1-3
"Do not let your heart be troubled; believe in God, believe also in Me. In My Father's house are many dwelling places; if it were not so, I would have told you; for I go to prepare a place for you. If I go and prepare a place for you, I will come again and receive you to Myself, that where I am, there you may be also.

John 16:33
These things I have spoken to you, so that in Me you may have peace. In the world you have tribulation, but take courage; I have overcome the world."

Joshua 1:9
Have I not commanded you? Be strong and courageous! Do not tremble or be dismayed, for the Lord your God is with you wherever you go."

Encouraging Scripture

Mark 11:24
Therefore I say to you, all things for which you pray and ask, believe that you have received them, and they will be granted you.

1 Peter 4:8
Above all, keep fervent in your love for one another, because love covers a multitude of sins.

Philippians 4:13
I can do all things through Him who strengthens me.

Philippians 4:6-7
Be anxious for nothing, but in everything by prayer and supplication with thanksgiving let your requests be made known to God. And the peace of God, which surpasses all comprehension, will guard your hearts and your minds in Christ Jesus.

Romans 8:31
What then shall we say to these things? If God is for us, who is against us?

Proverbs 17:17
A friend loves at all times,
And a brother is born for adversity.

Encouraging Scripture

Proverbs 18:10
The name of the Lord is a strong tower;
The righteous runs into it and is safe.

Proverbs 3:5-6
Trust in the Lord with all your heart
And do not lean on your own understanding.
In all your ways acknowledge Him,
And He will make your paths straight.

Proverbs 30:5
Every word of God is tested;
He is a shield to those who take refuge in Him.

Psalm 118:14
The Lord is my strength and song,
And He has become my salvation.

Psalm 119:50
This is my comfort in my affliction,
That Your word has revived me.

Psalm 34:8
 O taste and see that the Lord is good;
How blessed is the man who takes refuge in Him!

Encouraging Scripture

Psalm 16:5-8

The Lord is the portion of my inheritance and my cup;
You support my lot.
 The lines have fallen to me in pleasant places;
Indeed, my heritage is beautiful to me.
 I will bless the Lord who has counseled me;
Indeed, my mind instructs me in the night.
 I have set the Lord continually before me;
Because He is at my right hand, I will not be shaken.

Psalm 18:32-36

The God who girds me with strength
And makes my way blameless?
He makes my feet like hinds' feet,
And sets me upon my high places.
He trains my hands for battle,
So that my arms can bend a bow of bronze.
You have also given me the shield of Your salvation,
And Your right hand upholds me;
And Your gentleness makes me great.
You enlarge my steps under me,
And my feet have not slipped.

Psalm 27:14

Wait for the Lord;
Be strong and let your heart take courage;
Yes, wait for the Lord.

Encouraging Scripture

Psalm 27:1
The Lord is my light and my salvation;
Whom shall I fear?
The Lord is the defense of my life;
Whom shall I dread?

Psalm 46:1-3
God is our refuge and strength,
A very present help in trouble.
 Therefore we will not fear, though the earth should change
And though the mountains slip into the heart of the sea;
 Though its waters roar and foam,
Though the mountains quake at its swelling pride. Selah.

Psalm 55:22
Cast your burden upon the Lord and He will sustain you;
He will never allow the righteous to be shaken.

Psalm 28:7
The Lord is my strength and my shield;
My heart trusts in Him, and I am helped;
Therefore my heart exults,
And with my song I shall thank Him.

Psalm 37:4
Delight yourself in the Lord;
And He will give you the desires of your heart.

Encouraging Scripture

Psalm 121:1-8
I will lift up my eyes to the mountains;
From where shall my help come?
My help comes from the Lord,
Who made heaven and earth.
He will not allow your foot to slip;
He who keeps you will not slumber.
Behold, He who keeps Israel
Will neither slumber nor sleep.
The Lord is your keeper;
The Lord is your shade on your right hand.
The sun will not smite you by day,
Nor the moon by night.
The Lord will protect you from all evil;
He will keep your soul.
The Lord will guard your going out and your coming in
From this time forth and forever.

Psalm 31:24
Be strong and let your heart take courage,
All you who hope in the Lord.

Romans 15:4-5
For whatever was written in earlier times was written for our
instruction, so that through perseverance and the
encouragement of the Scriptures we might have hope. Now
may the God who gives perseverance and encouragement
grant you to be of the same mind with one another according
to Christ Jesus,

Encouraging Scripture

Psalm 34:4
I sought the Lord, and He answered me,
And delivered me from all my fears.

Romans 5:1
Therefore, having been justified by faith, we have peace with
God through our Lord Jesus Christ,

Psalm 55:22
Cast your burden upon the Lord and He will sustain you;
He will never allow the righteous to be shaken.

Romans 15:13
Now may the God of hope fill you with all joy and peace in
believing, so that you will abound in hope by the power of the
Holy Spirit.

Romans 8:38-39
For I am convinced that neither death, nor life, nor angels, nor
principalities, nor things present, nor things to come, nor
powers, nor height, nor depth, nor any other created thing,
will be able to separate us from the love of God, which is in
Christ Jesus our Lord.

James 4:8
Draw near to God and he will draw near to you

Final Thoughts

First, thank you so much for taking the time to read this book. It is my prayer that this has been a blessing to you and your family.

Secondly, if you have an opportunity to send me an e-mail with your thoughts, comments or suggestions, that would be very helpful.

Finally, I hope you were encouraged and strengthened by what you read.

paulbeersdorf@gmail.com

Blessings to you and your family!

Paul Beersdorf